T0044426

The Bible Unfiltered

Approaching Scripture on Its Own Terms

Other titles by Michael S. Heiser

The Unseen Realm:
Recovering the Supernatural Worldview of the Bible

Supernatural:
What the Bible Teaches about the Unseen
World—and Why It Matters

I Dare You Not to Bore Me with the Bible

The Bible Unfiltered

Approaching Scripture on Its Own Terms

Michael S. Heiser

LEXHAM PRESS

The Bible Unfiltered: Approaching Scripture on Its Own Terms

Copyright 2017 Lexham Press

Some material adapted with permission from content originally published in *Bible Study Magazine*.

Lexham Press, 1313 Commercial St., Bellingham, WA 98225
LexhamPress.com

Print ISBN 9781683590408
Digital ISBN 9781683590415

Lexham Editorial Team: Douglas Mangum and Danielle Thevenaz
Cover Design: Brittany Schrock
Typesetting: ProjectLuz.com

For all my faithful Naked Bible Podcast listeners

Contents

Introduction   1

PART ONE: INTERPRETING THE BIBLE RESPONSIBLY

1. Serious Bible Study Isn't for Sissies   7
2. Getting Serious—and Being Honest—about
   Interpreting the Bible in Context   11
3. Sincerity and the Supernatural   16
4. Let the Bible Be What It Is   19
5. Bad Bible Interpretation Really Can Hurt People   23
6. Unyielding Literalism: You Reap What You Sow   27
7. Everything in the Bible Isn't about Jesus   32
8. Bible Reading and Bible Memorization Are Not Bible Study   35
9. Marxism and Biblical Theology Aren't Synonyms   39
10. How to (Mis)Interpret Prophecy   44

PART TWO: OLD TESTAMENT

11. Did Yahweh Father Cain?   49
12. All Your Genesis Commentaries Are 8-Track Tapes   52
13. What's in a Name?   56
14. Lost at Sea   59
15. The Slave before "Elohim" in Exodus 21:1–6   62
16. The Angel of Yahweh in the Old Testament   67
17. Salvation in Old Testament Israel   77
18. Where the Wild (Demonic) Things Are   81
19. The Secret Things Belong to the Lord   84
20. The Ongoing Battle of Jericho   87
21. Scripture's Sacred Trees   91
22. Boaz—the Lawbreaker?   94
23. Of Mice and Manhood   97
24. Samuel's Ghost and Saul's Judgment   100
25. The Politics of Marriage   103
26. Defeating Ancient Foes   106
27. Yahweh and His Asherah   108
28. Angels Aren't Perfect   113
29. From Intercessors to Advocate   116

30. Jurassic Bible?   119
31. Proverbs: The Wisdom of Egypt?   124
32. Heap Burning Coals on Their Heads   129
33. Denial of the Afterlife   132
34. Solomon's Bride or Jesus' Bride?   135
35. Gog of the Supernatural North   138
36. Filtering God   141
37. God of Fire and Storm   144
38. Zechariah's Divine Messiah   147

PART THREE: NEW TESTAMENT

39. Mark's Use of Isaiah   153
40. Demons, Swine, and Cosmic Geography   157
41. Strange and Powerful Signs   160
42. Is Exorcism for Everyone?   163
43. The Word Was God   166
44. The Table of Nations and Acts 2   169
45. Paul's Missionary Goals   174
46. Divine Misdirection   178
47. Who is the God of This World?   181
48. New Testament Language of Spiritual
      Adoption and Sonship   185
49. The Lord, Who Is the Spirit   188
50. Paul, Puppies, and People with Tattoos   191
51. Watch Your Language!   194
52. No Longer Slaves   197
53. The Relationship of Baptism and Circumcision   200
54. Disarming the Powers of Darkness   204
55. Inspiration Was a Process, Not an Event   207
56. The Father of Lights   211
57. What Do Demons Believe about God?   214
58. Jesus, the Morning Star out of Jacob   218
59. Relying on Our Preconceptions   221
60. Jesus, Our Warrior   224

Abbreviations   229
Bibliography   231
Notes   235
Scripture Index   247

Introduction

Three years have passed since Lexham Press first decided to compile some of my *Bible Study Magazine* articles for publication as a book. The result was *I Dare You Not to Bore Me with the Bible*. In the introduction to that book I made the assertion that "truly understanding much of the Bible requires seeing it in its original context, not filtering it through a familiar tradition."[1] I'm more committed to that proposition now than I was even then. That idea is the motivation behind this second collection of articles, so the premise deserves some consideration.[2]

When we write or speak with the intention of being understood, we naturally consider our audience. Whether we're speaking to a toddler, writing an email to a parent, evaluating an employee, or clearing up a misunderstanding with a friend, we use vocabulary, style, and illustrative phrases drawn from *common* experiences, *mutual* intellectual perceptions, and *familiar* social situations. If we did not, we would have no right to expect to be understood. In fact, we would be misunderstood, perhaps quite disastrously. Our words derive from, and are shaped by, these factors. In other words, we understand each other to the extent that we share *life*—or, to put it less elegantly in a way only scholars can manage, to the extent that we share a cognitive framework.

The sort of connection between a writer and a reader that produces successful communication—with "success" being defined as the writer's intended thoughts being well comprehended by the reader—cannot occur without shared worldview and outlook. The biblical writers wanted to be understood. They did not write with the intention of miscommunicating. More fundamentally, God wanted his thoughts, character, and purposes grasped with clarity. He prepared and chose men to accomplish that task, not to insert obstacles to that task. This means that those of us living thousands of years after the words of Scripture were written face a predicament. We come from a different world. We did not share life with them. We are not of one mind in a multitude of ways.

The hard work of translation has made it possible to read the words of the biblical writers. But communication involves far more than taking words of one language and converting them into the words of another. Sharing outlook and worldview—life as it were—makes those words comprehensible. I can tell a Chinese friend that "abortion is a hot potato in America," but he'll never know what I mean by merely knowing the words "hot" and "potato" in English. This idiomatic expression can only be understood by experience within American culture or plenty of exposure to Americans. In another conversation my words may be intended to be understood metaphorically. I might refer to some object or concept whose symbolic, iconic meaning is what I wanted him to catch so that I might be understood. He needs me living in his head (that is, he needs to understand my worldview) to really fathom what I'm talking about.

It's true that some things in Scripture—often very important events and ideas—are communicated with simplicity and in ways that transcend this chronological chasm. But the reverse is also true. Many passages in Scripture are quite perplexing. More troubling is the fact that a good number of our traditional, presumed understandings do not align with what the writer likely intended at all. The correct response to this is not despair. While we can't understand everything in Scripture with perfect precision, we *can* understand a great deal once we connect to the worldview and outlook of the writers. It would be absurd to conclude that since it's impossible to achieve exhaustive comprehension of the Bible we shouldn't study it. Since you cannot know that everything you eat is entirely optimal for what your body needs at any given point should you stop eating?

We are blessed to have access to more information that connects us to the contexts of the biblical writers than ever before. My goal as a scholar is not only to alert you to the need for getting connected to those contexts, but to give you a head start. My prayer is that *The Bible Unfiltered* will do just that.

Michael S. Heiser
Bellingham, WA

Part One

Interpreting the Bible Responsibly

1

Serious Bible Study Isn't for Sissies

One of my favorite scholarly quotations about the hard work of seriously engaging the biblical text—what we popularly call Bible study—is that of the renowned Greek lexicographer, Frederick W. Danker (the "D" in BDAG).[1] Danker famously said that "scholars' tasks are not for sissies." He was right, and I'm grateful he was willing to say what needed to be said.

The truth about serious Bible study is that it isn't easy. It takes sustained time and effort, often measured in days, weeks, and months, to really grasp what a passage means (or probably means) and why. If Bible study doesn't seem like work to you, you aren't *really* doing it.

I realize that saying serious Bible study is work takes the pleasure out of it for some people. But presuming that you have to choose

> *If Bible study doesn't seem like work to you, you aren't really doing it.*

between enjoying the study of Scripture and attaining a more advanced grasp of it is a fallacy. People who are really good at anything or have a deep comprehension of a subject enjoy their mastery because they put in the work. Whether it's mastering an instrument, becoming a chef, or fielding countless ground balls in practice, people at the top of any given field only reached that station after thousands of hours of effort. People who make those sorts of sacrifices when it comes to the study of Scripture have counted the cost. They decided that the exertion wasn't going to deter them. They weren't sissies.

Do you really want to know more about Scripture than satisfies most? Do you really want a deep comprehension of this thing we call the word of God? If you do, here are some points of advice.

The goal of Bible study isn't to get a spiritual buzz.

First, let's get the obvious out of the way. Any student of Scripture who really believes the Bible is God's message to humanity will be emotionally moved from time to time at the wonder of why and how God maintains a loving interest in us. That's normal for someone who really understands the spiritual implications of Scripture. So I'm not suggesting emotional responses are antithetical to serious engagement with the Bible. What I am suggesting, though, is that if you're doing Bible study to *feel* a particular way, or get some spiritual high, then your Bible study is too self-focused.

Nowhere are we taught in the Bible to "search the Scriptures to feel a certain way." Ultimately, Scripture is about God—what he did, what he is doing, and what he will do—not about you. You'll never appreciate *God's* story if *your* story—and solving *your* problems—is what you focus on when you study Scripture. Comprehending God's story can go a long way toward addressing your problems, but the reverse will never be true. Serious Bible study that transcends self-therapy is about mastering the inspired text. You either want that or you don't. If you do, you'll be willing to put in the time and be willing to constantly reevaluate your work and your thinking.

Paying attention to detail and thinking clearly are not antithetical to loving Jesus.

Early in my own spiritual journey, I was consumed with knowing Scripture. I'd ask questions, listen to answers, and then follow up with more questions. Sometimes it irritated people. I recall several instances in church or home Bible studies where I was scolded about obsessing over the Bible. After all, I was told, the real point of Bible study was learning about Jesus and how to follow him.

I disagreed then and I still do. The answer to why women who had their periods were considered unclean (Lev 15:19–24), or what the Urim and Thummim were (Exod 28:30), or why some English translations of John 5 don't include verse 4 in the chapter have nothing to do with Jesus. The fact that they're in the Bible means they're just as inspired as any passage that is about Jesus.

Bible study is about learning what this thing we say is inspired actually means. Knowing what all its parts mean will give us a deeper appreciation for the salvation history of God's people, and the character of God. Jesus is the core component of all that, but there's a lot more to those things than the story of his life, death, and resurrection; his parables; and the Sermon on the Mount. If that was all God wanted us to know, he'd have given us only the four gospels. It's pretty evident he had more in mind.

9

The Spirit's guidance wasn't intended to serve as a cheat sheet.

If you've watched a baseball or football game on American television at some point, you no doubt have seen players either ask God for success or thank him for it. Athletes today regularly do things like point to the heavens after crossing home plate or finding themselves in the end zone. Some will bow in a short prayer. It's a nice sentiment and, for many, a testimony that transcends a token gesture.

But let's be honest. Unless that football player gets in shape and memorizes the playbook, all the pointing to heaven in the world isn't going to lead to success. You can say a short prayer on the mound or in the batter's box, but unless you can hit the curveball, you're going to fail—perhaps spectacularly.

It's the same in Bible study. All too often people who sincerely want the feeling of knowing Scripture aren't willing to put in the time it takes to get there. Instead, they'll take short cuts and then expect the Spirit to take up the slack. The assumption seems to be that the promise of the Spirit to guide us into truth means he'll excuse a lack of effort and give us the answers we need. The third person of the Trinity isn't the boy sitting next to you in high school that lets you cheat off his exam.

Rather than substitute the Spirit for personal effort, ask the Spirit for insight to expose flawed thinking (your own and that of whomever you're reading) when you're engaged in Bible study. The more of God's word you've devoted attention to, the more the Spirit has to work with.

2

Getting Serious—and Being Honest—about Interpreting the Bible in Context

Anyone interested in Bible study, from the new believer to the biblical scholar, has heard (and maybe even said) that if you want to correctly interpret the Bible, you have to interpret it *in context*. I'm certainly not going to disagree. But I have a question: What does that mean? Put another way, just what context are we talking about?

There are many contexts to which an interpreter needs to pay attention.

- **Historical context** situates a passage in a specific time period against the backdrop of certain events.
- **Cultural context** concerns the way people lived and how they thought about their lives and their world.
- **Literary context** focuses on how a given piece of biblical literature conforms (or not) to how the same type of literature was written during biblical times.

All of these are important—but they only flirt with the heart of the matter. There's a pretty clear element to this "context talk" that we're missing. It's time to get a firm grasp on something obvious. Believe it or not, it took years of study before I had it fixed in my head and my heart.

The Bible's True Context

As Christians, whether consciously or otherwise, we've been trained to think that the history of Christianity is the true context for interpreting the Bible. It isn't. That might be hard to hear, but Christian history and Christian thought is *not* the context of the biblical writers, and so it cannot be the correct context for interpreting what they wrote.

The proper context for interpreting the Bible is not the church fathers. They lived a thousand years or more after most of the Old Testament was written. Less than a half dozen of them could read Hebrew. The New Testament period was a century or more removed from important early theologians like Irenaeus and Tertullian; Augustine, arguably the most famous early church figure, lived three hundred years after the conversion of Paul.[1] That's more time than has elapsed since the founding of the United States. Also, many church fathers worked primarily with the Old Testament translated into Greek, Latin, or Syriac versions, so a good bit of their exegesis is translation-driven. Further, they were often responding to the intellectual issues of their own day when they wrote about Scripture, not looking back to the biblical context.

The farther down the timeline of history one moves, the greater the contextual gap becomes. The context for interpreting the biblical text is not the Catholic Church. It is not the rabbinic movements of Late Antiquity or the Middle Ages. It is not the Reformation—the time of Luther, Calvin, Zwingli, or the Anabaptists. It is not the time of the

Puritans. It is not evangelicalism in any of its flavors. It is not the modern world at all.[2]

So what is the proper context for interpreting the Bible? Here's the transparently obvious truth I was talking about: the proper context for interpreting the Bible is the context of the biblical writers—the context that produced the Bible. Every other context is alien or at least secondary.

Bridging the Context Gap

The biblical text was produced by people living in the ancient Near East and around the Mediterranean between the second millennium BC and the first century AD. To understand how biblical writers thought, we need to tap into that context. We need to get the worldview of the ancient world, shared by the biblical writers, into our heads.

As certain as this observation is, there is a pervasive tendency in the believing Church to filter the Bible through creeds, confessions, and denominational preferences. That's not a bad thing. It's a human thing. Creeds are useful for distilling important points of theology. But they are far from the whole counsel of God, and even farther from the biblical world. This is something to be aware of at all times.

Lest I be misunderstood, I'm not arguing that we should ignore our Christian forefathers. I'm also not saying that we're smarter. They were prodigious intellects. The problem isn't their brain power—it's that they were simply too removed from the world of the biblical writers and had little chance of bridging that gap.

It might sound odd, but we're actually in a better position than any of our spiritual forefathers in that respect. We live at a time when the languages of the major civilizations that flourished during the lifetimes of the biblical writers have been deciphered. We can tap into the intellectual and cultural output of those civilizations. That output is enormous—millions of words. We can recover the worldview context (their "cognitive framework" in scholar-speak) of the biblical writers as never before. The same is true of the New Testament writers because they inherited what had come before them and were part of a first century world two thousand years removed from us.

Think about it. How would anyone living a thousand years from now understand something you wrote unless they could get inside your head and see the world as you do? They'd need your frame of reference. They'd need to know what was going on in the wider world that potentially concerned, angered, encouraged, or depressed you. They'd need to understand the pop culture of your day to be able to parse why you're using this word and not that one, or to properly process an expression. There's no way to do that unless they recover your frame of reference. That is what it means to interpret in context.

The day I decided to commit myself to framing my study of Scripture in the context of the biblical world instead of any modern substitute was a day of liberation.

I know firsthand this is a hard lesson. It isn't easy to put the biblical context ahead of our traditions. But if we don't do that, we ought to stop talking about how important it is to interpret the Bible in context lest we be hypocrites. I can honestly say that the day I decided to commit myself to framing my study of Scripture in the context of the biblical world instead of any modern substitute was a day of liberation. It's what put me on a path to reading the Bible again— for the first time. You can do that, too. Don't believe me? Stay tuned.

3

Sincerity and the Supernatural

In the previous article, I noted that the right context for interpreting the Bible accurately isn't the history of Christianity in any of its creedal distillations or denominational forms. But I went even further—I said that the biblical context isn't *any* modern world context, period. The right context for understanding the Bible is the context that produced the Bible. That seems simple, but experience has taught me that commitment to this patently obvious truth isn't easy.

The biblical context includes its supernaturalism. The biblical writers believed in an active, animate spiritual world. That world was home to a lot more than the triune God, angels, Satan, and demons. It included other gods (i.e., the gods of the nations were not merely idols) and territorial spiritual beings that were not demons—and were, in fact, superior to demons.[1] It included what we think of as ghosts, who could appear visibly, and even physically, and communicate to the embodied living world of which they had once been a part (1 Sam 28:3-20). For the biblical writers, divine beings could eat, drink, fight, and produce offspring with humans (Gen 6:1-4; 18:1-8; 19:1-11; 32:22-32; Num 13:32-33; 2 Pet 2:4-10; Jude 6-7).

Facing Up to the Bible's "Weird" Passages

In the biblical worldview, the supernatural unseen realm had its own pecking order.[2] Scripture never says that such intelligent beings always had the same agenda, either. The members of the heavenly host were also created in God's image (the plurality language of Gen 1:26 isn't about the Trinity), so they possess free will, the ability to make decisions. Their acts and attitudes are not programmed and predestined. They believe they can defeat the plans of God, or at least forestall them indefinitely, at great pain to him and great cost to humanity (eternal and otherwise).

Let's face it—we just don't think like that. The above isn't the supernatural world of most Christian traditions. That doesn't matter if we're sincere about reading Scripture through the cognitive framework of its writers and original intended audience. But in many cases, especially in evangelical biblical scholarship, the supernatural thinking of the biblical writers has been something to explain away or avoid. I've seen it hundreds of times over the course of twenty years of sustained focused study as a biblical scholar. There are many creative ways to explain away what the text plainly says in various "weird" passages. But understanding Scripture isn't about making it palatable or comfortable to modern readers. It's about discerning what the biblical writer believed and was seeking to communicate to readers who thought the same way.

Understanding Scripture isn't about making it palatable or comfortable to modern readers.

Are We Sincere about Biblical Authority?

To be blunt, most Christians think themselves believers in the supernatural because they believe in the Trinity, Satan, angels, and demons. They profess Christ and believe in God—and that's the extent of what they truly think is real in terms of the supernatural. They affirm what they need to affirm to call themselves Christians. The rest is too scary or weird or seems simply superstitious.

When it comes to the supernatural, the question for every Christian who says they believe in biblical inspiration and authority to ask themselves is simple: How much of what biblical characters and writers believed about the supernatural world do I believe? Put negatively: How much of what biblical characters and writers believed about the supernatural world do I feel comfortable dismissing as a modern person? The answer to these questions will tell you how serious you are about biblical authority on such matters.

4

Let the Bible Be What It Is

As a biblical scholar, I'm often asked for advice on how to interpret the Bible. I could refer people to tools (like Logos Bible Software) and techniques for analyzing the original languages, even for people dependent on English.[1] But neither of those are my go-to answer. My own journey has convinced me there's one fundamental insight that, if faithfully observed, will help more than anything. It's the best piece of advice I can give you:

Let the Bible be what it is.

What do I mean? I'm suggesting that the path to real biblical understanding requires that we don't make the Bible conform to our traditions, our prejudices, our personal crises, or our culture's intellectual battles. Yes, you'll find material in Scripture that will help you resolve personal difficulties and questions. But you must remember that, while the Bible was written for us, it wasn't written to us. What they wrote is still vital for our lives today, but we can only accurately discern the message if we let them speak as they spoke.

This advice of course dovetails with my previous article about getting serious and being honest about the oft-repeated mantra "the Bible needs to be interpreted in context." That article was about recognizing all contexts—including the history of Christianity—that post-date the biblical world are foreign to the Bible. The right contexts for interpreting the Bible are those in which the Bible was written. You can't let the Bible be what it is if you're filtering it through a set of experiences and ideas (a "cognitive framework") that would have been incomprehensible to the biblical writers.

> *You can't let the Bible be what it is if you're filtering it through a set of experiences and ideas that would have been incomprehensible to the biblical writers.*

A Firm Grasp of the Obvious

I know that, on the surface, what I'm saying amounts to having a firm grasp of the obvious. But if it were easy to do—and if it was the norm—I'd be writing about something else. It isn't and it hasn't been. But it certainly needs to be, at least if we don't want to be pretenders when it comes to respecting God's decision to produce Scripture when he did and through whom he chose.

Many illustrations come to mind of the importance of letting the Bible be what it is. The supernaturalist worldview I talked about before, which is the focus of my books *The Unseen Realm* and *Supernatural,* is one example.[2] I'll return to that illustration later. I want to offer two others.

What about the pre-scientific cosmology of the Bible? I've written about the ancient Hebrew conception of the universe in the *Faithlife Study Bible*.[3] For the biblical writers, the earth was flat and round, supported by pillars (2 Sam 22:8) and surrounded by water (Gen 1:10); the water was held in place by the edges of the solid dome ("expanse"; "firmament") that covered the earth (Gen 1:6; Prov 8:27–28). The people God chose to write about the fact that he created everything were not writing science because they couldn't—and God, of course, knew that. Instead of pressing Genesis into a debate with Darwin or making it cryptically convey the truths of quantum physics, we should let it be what it is so it can accomplish the goals for which God inspired it—to assert the fact of a Creator and our accountability to him. Rather than fight the critics on grounds they choose, we ought to insist that they explain why it makes any sense to criticize the Bible for not being what it wasn't intended to be. Following such absurd logic, perhaps we should expect them to criticize their dog for not being a cat or their son for not being a daughter. Their attack is patently absurd. But we endorse it when we make the Bible a modern science book instead of letting it be what it is— what God intended.

Truth That Transcends Culture

The same problem persists when we try to deny that the Old Testament is patriarchal, or that parts of the Mosaic Law are biased against women. Some are because that was their culture. God didn't hand down a new culture for particular use in Scripture. He didn't demand that the writers he chose change their worldview before he'd use them. The biblical material simply reflects the cultural attitudes of the people who wrote it.

Again, all this is obvious—but so many students of Scripture seem to approach such issues with the assumption that the Bible endorses a culture. God wasn't trying to endorse a culture from the first millennium BC or the first century AD for all time and in all places among all peoples. The reason ought to be apparent: God knew that the truths he wanted to get across through the biblical writers would transcend all cultures. Endorsing the prejudices the writers grew up with wasn't what God had in mind. Some parts of Scripture reveal culture simply as part of Israel's history. Others focus on behavior. With respect to the latter, God let the writers be who they were (i.e., he knew what he was getting when he chose them for their task), knowing they were capable of communicating timeless principles of conduct by means of their culture.

The point is that letting the Bible be what it is not only helps us interpret Scripture accurately, but it has unexpected apologetic value. Taking Scripture on its own terms helps our focus and fends off distractions. When Scripture is rightly understood, its relevance will also be clear.

5

Bad Bible Interpretation Really Can Hurt People

Anyone who teaches the word of God wants people excited about exploring Scripture. Ultimately, you want to turn listeners into competent students so that they can teach others. Along the way you have to deal with a lot of mistaken methods and conclusions. But so what? Hey—having folks engaged in studying the Bible is more important than what they actually think they see in it. It's no concern that what most Christians think is "digging deep" is barely scratching the surface of a passage or a topic. I'll take one misguided Bible student over a hundred straight-laced, passive, ecclesiastically-correct "believers" who never open a Bible anywhere else but church. At least those are the sorts of things I've told myself for a long time. If I'm honest, though, I've had doubts about the wisdom of my position. I still do.

I've run across a lot of bad Bible interpretation over the years. The problem isn't just the Internet. Granted, most of what passes for Bible teaching online could be aggregated under the banner of the "P.T. Barnum School of the Bible." Unfortunately, a lot of poor thinking about Scripture has been published for popular consumption in the Church— and consumed it is.

But is it really harmful? Most of it isn't destructive. It won't do anything worse than keep those who buy into it ignorant and never able to move on to what they might really discover. And I've seen a few instances where bad Bible interpretation has even been helpful. Because of the sorts of things I do—especially writing paranormal fiction and maintaining two blogs on strange stuff that people believe—I often encounter people with terribly misguided ideas about the Bible and its meaning. My offbeat "ministry" produces all sorts of, shall we say, interesting email. Many people who contact me are Christians with genuine testimonies who've had an unusual, frightening experience, or who've spent too much time watching *Ancient Aliens* on the Fantasy (er, History) Channel. After their pastor or another friend who's ill-equipped to talk about what's causing their spiritual crisis tells them they need counseling (or worse), they have a decision to make: dump Christianity or find a way to process what's disturbing them using the Bible. I've heard some of the most absurd Bible interpretation imaginable emerge from those sorts of struggles, but it often keeps people pursuing the Lord. So be it. In these circumstances, the last thing that's needed is a biblical scholar-bully destroying the interpretations that keep people in the faith. It's far better to maintain some relationship and build some trust. Maybe down the road we can have a talk about the fact that the Tower of Babel really wasn't a Stargate.

Truly Destructive Bible Interpretation

But some Bible interpretation is truly damaging—and on a wide scale. For that sort of harm you need professionals—people who are supposed to know better because they have degrees or are in positions of spiritual leadership.

Perhaps the most egregious example is racism. Since the Age of Exploration (16th century) on through the eras of European empire and colonization, the racism that was an inextricable part of those centuries can be laid at the feet of the Church. Though it may make you flinch, it's true—and I'm not launching into some ludicrous left-wing propagandistic screed. It's pretty simple and, on its own terms, very understandable, though the coherence of how it all came about is no excuse.[1]

In the sixteenth century, as Europeans ventured for the first time across the Atlantic and deepened their penetration east into the "Indies," they encountered people and places that were not part of the biblical world. The place that would be called North America was not India or China, places that Europeans had been exposed to earlier. How did they get here? The Bible said nothing about them. Things didn't get any more comfortable in the eighteenth and nineteenth centuries after the decipherment of the literary language of ancient India (Sanskrit). In a shocking twist, Sanskrit turned out to be from the same language family as classical Latin and Greek (Indo-European), the intellectual bedrock of European civilization. Sanskrit texts revealed a much longer human history than that of the Bible. And the physical evidence of a civilization much older than the patriarchs gave weight to that history.

The cumulative impact of all these discoveries was that the Bible no longer looked like it had any claim on being special. To make the crisis even more acute, in 1859 Charles Darwin published *On the Origin of Species*.[2] In the wake of that bombshell, the alternative stories of creation in Sanskrit and the discoveries of people in the New World who shouldn't have been there (because the Bible didn't mention them) gave opponents of the Bible all the ammunition they needed. The Bible was not only wrong, but inferior. After all, it was such a Jewish book.

It's no accident that this was the era that produced theories about how all races not European (especially blacks and Semitic peoples) were inferior to the "more pure" Europeans. Defenders of the Bible couldn't argue there; instead they did their best to make the Bible support those things. The era produced "scholarly" defenses of how the sin of Ham produced the black peoples, or how Cain's wife proved there were co-Adamic races in antiquity, inferior to Adam, who wasn't Jewish by the way, or that Jesus wasn't really a Jew but an Aryan, a Sanskrit term for the high born. Other interpretive leaps were used to justify older suspicions of Jews as Christ killers whose disinheritance by God had subordinated them to the civilization that had embraced Christianity—the Europeans. But at least the Bible wasn't left behind in its "accurate" understanding of history. It still deserved its high status. And so the Bible was "saved" through horrific Bible interpretation. And we're still living with the results since this was all brought to American shores.

So yes, sometimes bad Bible interpretation is truly destructive—with effects lasting generations. This is yet another illustration why we need to get serious about interpreting the Bible in its own context, not against the backdrop of our own modern questions. The tragic baptism of racism was completely unnecessary. But there it is.

6

Unyielding Literalism:
You Reap What You Sow

Now we've established that bad Bible interpretation really can be harmful. I mentioned earlier that I'm exposed to more than my fair share of interpretive incoherence because I'm known on the Internet for my paranormal fiction and for blogging on strange things people believe about the Bible and the ancient world. But that earlier article was about how historical circumstances produced challenges to biblical veracity and authority. Unfortunately, sometimes Bible believers have no one but themselves to blame for making the content of Scripture seem utterly absurd.

Recently, I've had the dispiriting experience of fielding several emails asking me to inject some sanity into the new flat earth movement circulating among Christians. Yes—you read that correctly: there's a growing cadre of "Bible teachers" busily contending for the faith by teaching their followers (in church and online) that the Bible requires us to believe the earth is flat. This idea is related to another

There's a growing cadre of "Bible teachers" busily contending for the faith by teaching their followers that the Bible requires us to believe the earth is flat.

"Bible fact" that is experiencing a revival: geocentrism, the idea that the earth is the center of our solar system, not the sun.[1] "Biblical geocentrism" is based on the hyper-literal interpretation of verses like Psalm 104:5 (the sun and other planets must revolve around the earth since the earth cannot be moved).

Now, I know what you're thinking. What about space travel? Satellites sent into orbit that enable (dare I say) global communication? Airline flight patterns that use the curvature of the earth to cheat passengers out of extra frequent flyer miles (okay, maybe that isn't the carrier's motivation)? The truth is these are conspiracies contrived by people who hate the Bible. That's what science does ... make up lies to cover up the fact that the Bible has the truth about how God created the earth. Sigh.

Sanctified Brainwashing

By what process of hermeneutical alchemy is all this possible? It's actually pretty simple: hyper-literalism. The sanctified flat-earthers have blindly presumed that the Bible's pre-scientific cosmology—which is well known to Old Testament scholars—has to be taken as a literal reality that trumps basic science (and human experience) or else biblical inspiration and inerrancy have to be rejected. This thinking is deeply flawed.

The Bible's pre-scientific cosmology is what it is because God decided to prompt people who lived in a pre-scientific age to produce the books of the Bible, not because the earth is really round and flat with a solid dome over it.[2] The flat-earthers and geocentrists sort of skip the dome part, unless they deny the lunar landings and the existence of the international space station. God didn't ask the people he picked to be something they weren't (modern scientists who understood celestial mechanics). He prompted them via his Spirit to tell some important truths: all we know was created by God—including us—and so we are accountable to him and dependent on him for life beyond this terrestrial existence. The biblical writers didn't need a modern science education to communicate, through their own worldview frame of reference and symbolic metaphors well known throughout the ancient world (their cultural context), who the true Creator was and why it mattered. That's taking the Bible for what it is and interpreting it in light of its own context, not ours. But too many Christians have been brainwashed into thinking that absolute, uncompromising literalism is a synonym for believing in inspiration and inerrancy. It isn't—and never has been throughout the entire history of believing Christianity.

Literalism as Idolatry

I've been a Christian for 35 years. For most of that time my church context has been either fundamentalism (my early years as a believer) or, what I'll call for convenience, popular evangelicalism that divorces itself from a reformed or creedal heritage. Both of those Christian sub-cultures exalt the "literal" interpretation of the Bible, especially when it comes to creation and prophecy. Granted, the notion that the Bible teaches a flat earth isn't common to those contexts. But over-emphasis on biblical literalism has a cost. Literalism can become idolatry. During my teaching career I've had students espouse a number of preposterous Bible teachings, among them:

- Babies are really stored in a man's sperm (the Hebrew word for "seed" [zr ʿ] refers to children and is never used of women); genetics is a lie (Gen 13:16; zr ʿ = offspring)
- The Bible teaches teleportation (Acts 8:39–40)
- Flying saucers are piloted by angels (Ezek 1; Zech 5:5–8)
- Animals could talk in Eden (Gen 3)

I could extend the list, but I think you get the point. But here's a point that's less obvious that you might miss: when we unquestioningly teach Bible students that literalness is next to godliness, we teach them to think poorly. Don't believe me? Read on.

What Does "Literal" Mean Anyway?

Many readers have heard the old bromide in defense of literal Bible interpretation: "When the plain sense makes sense, seek no other sense." It's pithy. If you don't think too much about it, it might even sound like it makes sense. It's actually not helpful.

It might sound odd, but "literal interpretation" needs to be interpreted. The meaning is far from clear. Consider the word "water." What does it "literally" mean? Is it a noun or a verb? In either case, what exactly is its "plain sense"? Here are some options. As a noun, "water" can be:

- a chemical compound (H_2O)
- a liquid beverage ("I'd like some water")
- a natural body of water ("look at all that water"), but which kind?
  - an ocean
  - a sea

- a lake
- a pond
- a river
- a stream
- a creek
- an inlet

As a verb, "water" can mean:
- to irrigate ("water the fields")
- to provide hydration ("he watered the cattle")
- to salivate ("my mouth watered")
- to cry ("his eyes watered")

So which of the above is the "literal" meaning? Which one is the "plain" meaning? That's the point. They're all plain. What distinguishes them is context and metaphor. Things get even more interesting when you move into metaphorical meanings for water—and metaphorical meaning can be exactly what context requires. "Water" can be used metaphorically for a life source, purification, transformation, motion, or danger. The metaphors work because of the physical properties of water—and still describe real things. Non-literal doesn't mean "not real." And as the saga of sanctified geocentrism tells us, devotion to literalism won't necessarily produce accurate—or even coherent— Bible interpretation.

7

Everything in the Bible
Isn't about Jesus

If you've been a Christian for very long or were raised in a Christian church, chances are that you've heard that the Bible is really all about Jesus. That cliché has some truth to it, but it's misleading.

The truth is that there's a lot in the Bible that *isn't* about Jesus. Procedures for diagnosing and treating leprosy (Lev 13:1–14:57) aren't about Jesus. Laws forbidding people who've had sex or lost blood (Lev 15) from entering sacred space aren't about Jesus. The spiritual, social, and moral corruption in the days of the judges (Judg 17–21) wasn't put in the Bible to tell us about Jesus. The Tower of Babel incident (Gen 11:1–9) doesn't point to Jesus. When Ezra commanded Jews who'd returned from exile to divorce the Gentile women they'd married (Ezra 9–10), he wasn't foreshadowing anything about Jesus.

The point is straightforward: No Israelite would have thought of a messianic deliverer when reading these or many other passages. No New Testament writer alludes to them and many other portions of Scripture to explain who Jesus was or what he said.

Why Is This Idea So Prevalent?

In my experience, the prevailing motivation seems to be to encourage people to read their Bible. That's a good incentive. But I've also come across other factors, namely that it serves as an excuse to avoid the hard work of figuring out what's really going on in many passages. People are taught to extrapolate what they read to some point of connection with the life and ministry of Jesus—no matter how foreign to Jesus the passage appears. Imagination isn't a sound hermeneutic. Not only does it lack boundaries that prevent very flawed interpretations (and even heresies), but it makes Scripture serve our ability to be clever. Recognizing the inaccuracy of this assumption is important for some simple but important reasons.

First, if we filter passages that aren't about Jesus through something Jesus did and said, we won't have any hope of understanding what those passages were actually about. Nothing in Scripture is there accidentally. The Bible is an intelligent creation. Our task as those with a high view of Scripture is to discern why God wanted a given passage in the Bible in the first place.

Second, the assumption can lead to minimizing or ignoring passages in which we can't clearly see Jesus. Since Jesus is central to God's sovereign plan of salvation, passages that don't

> *If we filter passages that aren't about Jesus through something Jesus did and said, we won't have any hope of understanding what those passages were actually about.*

add some detail about his teachings or the gospel story are considered peripheral or optional. Why bother spending serious time in a passage that "doesn't matter" for having eternal life? Giving us the Bible as we have it was a providential, intentional decision on God's part. We either believe that's true and act accordingly (i.e., studying the whole counsel of God), or we'll act as though God's decision was random and unintelligent.

Third, becoming skilled at seeing Jesus in places where he isn't can discourage others from Bible study or lead others under one's spiritual charge to believe we have special (even authoritative) insight. When "Jesus stuff" isn't obvious in a given passage and we've been taught that it's somehow all about him, it's easy to just give up and let pastors and others tell us what they "see." People shut off their brains when they are led to believe they can't think well about Scripture.

The bottom line is that we can talk about the inspiration and authority of the Bible all day long and still fall prey to marginalizing its content with familiar clichés that let us off the hook from doing the hard work of interpretation. While the drama of the biblical epic ultimately leads to Jesus, he isn't the ultimate focal point of every passage. That's homiletical flair, not the reality of the text.

8

Bible Reading and Bible Memorization Are Not Bible Study

Let's get the obvious out of the way. You should read your Bible. You should also commit Scripture to memory. Both spiritual disciplines are axiomatic for Christians. But neither one is Bible study. I'll explain what I mean by taking one at a time.

Reading Is Casual—Study Isn't

Reading the Bible is not where your engagement with the Bible ends. It's where it begins, or at least where it ought to begin. But over the course of my teaching career I've been dragged kicking and screaming to the realization that many Christians think the act of reading Scripture is to be equated with studying Scripture. That simply isn't the case.

> Reading the Bible is not where your engagement with the Bible ends. It's where it begins.

Reading is casual, something done for pleasure. The motivation is personal enjoyment or enrichment, not mastery of the content. We read Scripture to be reminded of God's story in human history and the life lessons that story provides for our own lives and our relationship with God. Bible reading is inherently devotional and low maintenance.

Bible study, on the other hand, involves concentration and exertion. We have an intuitive sense that study requires some sort of method or technique, and probably certain types of tools or aids. When we study the Bible we're asking questions, thinking about context, forming judgments, and looking for more information.

It's not hard to illustrate the difference. Practically anyone could manage to make a cup of coffee, but they're not baristas. We know instinctively that both perform the same basic task, but what distinguishes the barista is a lot of time, effort, research, and experience in learned technique. It's the same with Bible study.

Let's say you and your friend were from the moon and didn't know what coffee was. You're only mildly interested in the topic, so you decide to look it up in a dictionary. You read that coffee is "a popular beverage made from the roasted and pulverized seeds of a coffee plant." Good enough. You learned something. But your friend wants to know more—a lot more. How is coffee made? What's the process? Is there more than one process? Is there more than one kind of coffee bean? Where are the beans grown? Does that make any difference in color, aroma, or flavor? How is coffee different than tea? If it's a popular beverage, how much is consumed? Does consumption vary by country? State? Gender? Age? IQ? Maybe your friend doesn't need to discover caffeine. But you get the point. Study requires passion and commitment; reading is much less intense.

Memorization Isn't Thoughtful Analysis

When I was freshman in Bible college, one of my professors was something of a zealot for Bible memorization. During the semester he had us memorize 150 verses—with punctuation. I had an excellent short-term memory, so the feat wasn't that hard. While the discipline of that class was good for me, I have to be honest. I never learned what any of the verses meant in that class.

Being able to recollect a verse with precision does not mean you understand it. You could memorize your tax forms, but that isn't going to provide answers to any confusion that may arise from what they say. It also won't turn you into an accountant or an IRS agent. It's the same with Scripture. I could memorize the entire Bible, but how does that nurture my comprehension?

Real Bible study demands analysis and thinking. For example, you could easily commit the following sentence to memory: "New Study of Obesity Looks for Larger Test Group." Knowing what the words mean, though, takes some reflection (and a sense of humor).

Real Bible study demands analysis and thinking.

Many things we read, especially in the Bible, aren't as easy to parse as this funny headline. Many Christians will have memorized Ephesians 2:8–9 (LEB):

> For by grace you are saved through faith, and this is not from yourselves, it is the gift of God; it is not from works, so that no one can boast.

How many of us have bothered to ask the obvious question: What is the gift of God in this verse? Is it grace? Faith? Both? Something else? How would we know? Memorizing these verses is a good idea, but understanding what they mean is even better.

9

Marxism and Biblical Theology Aren't Synonyms

I'm a biblical scholar by training, but what most people don't realize is that I'm also a political junkie. My undergraduate degree is actually in History and Political Science. Since one of my graduate degrees is in history (albeit ancient history), I was able to teach western civilization at the college level to help support myself through graduate school. I've also taught U.S. History at a local community college. But while my interest in political discourse is high, I also have to confess to being an American political atheist—I don't put my faith in any political party. The answer to the nation's problems—to those plaguing a beleaguered world—is the kingdom of God, not a kingdom made by human hands, even American ones.

Why am I telling you this? It's to make the point that, though my PhD is in biblical studies, I'm not a newbie when it comes to political theory. My interests intersect in an area of Christian thinking that is becoming all too trendy: the notion that the New Testament supports Marxism.

This thought is hermeneutically inept for a number of reasons. It shows a fundamentally flawed biblical theology of poverty and care for the poor, conflates the gospel with socioeconomic concerns, ignores overt anti-Marxist statements by Jesus and the apostles, and misrepresents communist political theory. In short, it manifests ignorance on multiple fronts.

The Old Testament

The Old Testament makes certain elements of any discussion of our topic pretty clear.[1] Several biblical figures of high spiritual character have considerable wealth. The most obvious example is likely Abraham (Gen 24:34–35). Two of the Ten Commandments presuppose private property and criminalize its theft (Exod 20:15; Deut 5:21). Wealth is the fruit of labor (Prov 10:4; 13:4). Inherited wealth is also not condemned (Deut 21:16; Prov 19:14).

The biblical world knew poverty all too well. The Old Testament has a wide range of words describing poverty and the poor. But what do these terms indicate about the status of the poor? That is, what kinds of poverty does the Old Testament describe? Poverty had various causes in the Bible. The most common were warfare (foreign invasion), famine and drought, laziness, and being victimized by the unscrupulous.

What God hates isn't wealth—it's the abuse of the poor by the wealthy.

Does the Bible tell us that being wealthy is inherently unjust, automatically leads to injustice, or necessarily causes injustice? Anyone spending some serious time in the biblical text will learn that the answer to this question is no. Wealth is not an inherent evil according to biblical theology. What God hates isn't wealth—it's the abuse of the poor by those who, for example, extort them, manipulate them, or with-hold legal justice from them (Isa 3:14–15; 32:7; Amos 2:6–7; 5:12; Jer 5:28).

The question of context is also crucial. I would invite readers to read the short essay by Jon Levenson, "Poverty and the State in Biblical Thought."[2] Levenson is a Jewish biblical scholar. His article is important for helping us think about the relationship of the Israelite state to poverty as it's discussed in the Hebrew Bible. One of Levenson's insights is significant:

> The laws which protect the poor, then, are addressed to the individual and the clan, the local, highly organic unit of social organization. These laws are, thus, religious commandments, rather than state policy. They are obligations established by God and owed directly to the poor and not to the government as a mediator between rich and poor.[3]

The crucial point here is that the biblical call to care for the poor is not one that calls for that care to come from the authority of a state with coercive power. It is a call to individuals who seek to please God.

The New Testament

Jesus and the apostles got their theology about poverty from the Hebrew Bible. While, in Jesus' words, there will always be poor (John 12:8)—and so, unequal economic classes—God doesn't disdain the poor. Instead, he is displeased when they are oppressed by the wealthy (e.g., Deut 24:14; Prov 14:31; Zech 7:10; James 2:6).

Still, some careless thinkers believe the New Testament endorses Marxism. Acts 2:42–45 is often used as a proof text for people who presume the New Testament teaches this.

> [42] And they were devoting themselves to the teaching of the apostles and to fellowship, to the breaking of bread and to prayers. ... [44] And all who believed were in the same place, and had everything in common. [45] And they began selling their possessions and property, and distributing these things to all, to the degree that anyone had need. (LEB)

One of Marxism's famous slogans—"From each according to his ability, to each according to his need"—seems to fit this passage in Acts 2. But that takes Marxism and Acts 2 out of context. Marxist interpreters of Acts 2 miss the obvious fact that everything we read in that passage was *voluntary*. There was no all-powerful state (or religious authority) demanding redistribution of income and wealth. In Acts 5 believers were voluntarily selling property and distributing the proceeds among the believers. Even when Ananias and his wife sinned by deceptively withholding part of a property sale, Peter scolded, "And after it was sold, was it not at your disposal?" There is no coercion in this picture.

Acts 2 is also no justification for Marxist theory as an "application" of the passage for another reason: it would contradict the teaching of Jesus. It was Jesus who called for the separation of the church and state, who spoke of the kingdom of heaven as distinct from the state (Matt 22:21).

Food for Thought

In my experience, Christians who get warm, fuzzy feelings about Marxism have a genuine concern for the poor, but then they filter the New Testament through a very skewed understanding of both the Bible and the philosophy of Karl Marx. This post is about the former error, but the latter is just as readily apparent to anyone who has read Marx or Friedrich Engels, Marx's co-author for their classic statement, *The Communist Manifesto* (1848 political). Both were anti-Semitic. Their economic theory was designed to foment violent revolution, not care for the poor. It was Engels who said "Political liberty is sham-liberty, the worst possible slavery."[4]

It's easy to spot the glaring inconsistencies when people ignorant of biblical theology (including Christians) assume the Bible approves Marxism. But biblical theology doesn't endorse a lot of what we see in capitalism today either. Scripture is clear that wealth is not for hoarding or cultivating an aura of superiority. God wants wealth used to bless people. We as Christians

> *Scripture is clear that wealth is not for hoarding or cultivating an aura of superiority. God wants wealth used to bless people.*

violate Jesus' teaching about the separation of church and state when we forsake the care of the poor in tangible ways, presuming that the state will act on our behalf. In biblical theology, care for others is a personal spiritual duty, not something to be handed off to a secular authority. But that is basically what we do. We presume the state will act as the church should—as *we* should. That theology is just as bad as pretending the Bible teaches Marxism.

10

How to (Mis)Interpret Prophecy

There's no shortage of advice on how to interpret the Bible. One maxim that I've already mentioned advises, "When the plain sense makes sense, seek no other sense."[1] I've heard it quoted when it comes to biblical prophecy—encouraging people to interpret literally, at face value. Although that sounds like good advice, some New Testament writers didn't get the memo.

One of the most well-known examples of a non-literal reading appears in Acts 15 when the apostle James quotes Amos 9:11–12:

Acts 15:16–18	Amos 9:11–12
[16] After this I will return, and I will rebuild	[11] In that day I will raise up
the tent of David that has fallen;	the booth of David that is fallen
I will rebuild its ruins, and I will restore it,	and repair its breaches, and raise up its ruins and rebuild it as in the days of old,

[17] that	[12] that they may possess
the remnant of **mankind**[1]	the remnant of **Edom**[2]
may seek the Lord,	
and all the Gentiles	and all the nations
who are called by	who are called by my
my name,	name,"
says the Lord,	declares the Lord
who makes these things	who does this.
[18] known from of old.'	

In the Amos prophecy, God promises to one day "raise up the booth of David and repair its breaches, and raise up its ruins, and rebuild it." Hearing the language of repair and rebuilding, we might think of a physical structure. "Booth" (*sukkah*) is a word used for tents at the Feast of Booths (Lev 23:34). Reading literally, we might think that the tabernacle, still used in David's day and brought into the temple after it was built by Solomon, might be the focus of the prophecy.

Many interpret Amos 9 this way, believing the passage describes the rebuilding of the temple in Jerusalem in the end times. The "possession" of Edom and the nations who are destined to call the Lord their God would seem to fit that context.

But Luke, the writer of Acts, doesn't interpret the passage that way. He doesn't take it "plainly" or literally. In Acts 15, he describes the fledgling church gathering in Jerusalem to hear that Paul and Barnabas had taken the gospel to Gentiles, who had embraced it. Peter and James came to their defense. To prove the momentous event had been prophesied in the Old Testament, James quoted Amos 9:11–12. James (and the writer, Luke) understood the language of building and repairing to refer to a person—the resurrected Jesus, the son of David. They also don't refer to "the remnant of Edom" but instead "the remnant of mankind."

James and Luke used the Septuagint, the Greek translation of the Old Testament. The Hebrew version of the prophecy had "Edom" (Hebrew *'edom*), but the Septuagint reads "mankind" (reading the Hebrew as *'adam*). The words share the same consonants but are otherwise entirely different.

The switch to "mankind" fits the occasion of this meeting as well as the ministry of Paul and Barnabas. The Gentiles—all the nations of mankind, not just Israel—are now accepting the gospel. But that is not how the passage read in Hebrew. The interpretation by James and Luke is not a literal one, but an abstract or "spiritual" one, based on a different reading from a translation.

The interpretation by James and Luke is not a literal one, but an abstract or "spiritual" one, based on a different reading from a translation.

Did James and Luke misread the Bible, then? Not necessarily. The "remnant of Edom" could be considered an abstract reference to "non-elect" people: Remember that the Edomites were descendants of Esau (Gen 36:1), who surrendered his birthright (Gen 25). Therefore, the non-literal translation of "mankind" in the Septuagint version of Amos 9:11 is within the realm of accurate meaning.

Comparing these passages illustrates important lessons: Interpreting biblical prophecy cannot be distilled to a simple maxim, and everything cannot be taken literally. The New Testament shows us otherwise.

Part Two

Old Testament

11

Did Yahweh Father Cain?

Christians are often taught to interpret the Bible literally. In Part One, we looked at some of the problems that can come out of overemphasizing literal interpretation, but I should point out that most people who advocate literalism do so to prevent self-serving or idiosyncratic interpretations. If we interpret the text at face-value, so the idea goes, we'll more often than not be interpreting Scripture correctly. This approach—though well-intentioned—isn't always the best strategy, for several reasons. One is that the most straight-forward reading can produce bizarre outcomes.

Genesis 4:1 is a case in point: "Now Adam knew Eve his wife, and she conceived and bore Cain, saying, 'I have gotten a man with the help of the Lord.'" We might look at this verse and see nothing amiss, but the English translation is concealing a controversial problem. In Hebrew, Eve says, "*qanithi ish eth-YHWH*."[1] The English words "the help of" were supplied by the translator of the ESV; they are not represented in the Hebrew text.

In addition, the Hebrew verb *qanah* (the basic form of the word *qanithi*, translated "I have gotten" in the ESV) else-where can speak of creating. For example, it is the verb in the psalmist's famous statement about God's role in his birth: "For you formed (*qanah*) my inward parts; you knitted me together in my mother's womb" (Ps 139:13).

Insisting on the *most straightforward reading* of Genesis 4:1 easily produces an interpretation that has Eve saying, "I have created (or procreated) a man with Yahweh." While this translation might sound very odd to our ears, certain cults and religious sects held the view that Yahweh had a sexual relationship with Eve.[2] In one respect, such a translation is a gross misreading of the text, as the verse begins with a clear statement that Eve's sexual partner— and therefore the father of Cain—was Adam ("Adam knew Eve his wife, and she conceived and bore Cain"). But that doesn't resolve what the second half of the verse means to say.

> *Certain cults and religious sects held the view that Yahweh had a sexual relationship with Eve.*

The verb *qanah* is not among the Hebrew words used most frequently to describe conception and childbirth (such as *harah* and *yalad*). In fact, this meaning for *qanah* is rare. Most Hebrew scholars believe that the writer chose to use *qanah* in Gen 4:1 to produce wordplay, as it sounds a lot like the Hebrew name for Cain: *qayin*. Consequently, the second part of the verse was not intended to describe Eve procreating with Yahweh, especially since the first part has just made clear that Adam was Cain's father.

Statements elsewhere in the Bible—particularly several made by women who had difficulty bearing children— confirm the problem with taking Gen 4:1 too literally. Sarah, who clearly was unable to have children because of her age (Gen 18:11–12), knew that Yahweh had enabled her to have Isaac (Gen 18:13–15; 21:6–7). Hannah credited Yahweh with the birth of Samuel after she had been barren for many years (1 Sam 1:19–20).

Like these other women, Eve's statement that she had "created a man with the LORD"—after becoming pregnant by Adam—is an idiomatic expression: She is crediting God for blessing her with the mystery of childbirth. Translations of Gen 4:1 like the ESV express this idea correctly. Eve believed that God had played a role in bringing Cain into the world.

12

All Your Genesis Commentaries Are 8-Track Tapes

We've all heard the old saying that certain things get better with age—wine, cheese, common sense. Anyone who's watched *Antiques Roadshow* also knows that the longer you have something that there's a demand for—real estate, investments, fine art, a popular car—the more value it will accrue. Unfortunately, the reverse is true for many of the most popular tools for biblical study. They're often more like tech gear—they get worse with age and sometimes become totally obsolete.

Commentaries are one of the tools that don't get better with the passage of time. The reasons are pretty simple. Biblical scholars are like experts in any field. They keep thinking and researching. The data of biblical studies increase and improve. Archaeology produces more discoveries of relevance. Computer technology makes ancient language analysis more thorough (and faster). Information becomes more accessible and searchable. It's no exaggeration to say that what scholars had access to 100 years ago is literally a fraction of what's available to you today using only a smartphone. In terms of what previous generations were capable of analyzing in a lifetime we can surpass with a few hours of effort.

I work for the world's leading Bible software company, so I'm used to the staggering realities of the modern world for biblical studies. But the truth I'm talking about today was brought home to me in a direct way only recently. My book *The Unseen Realm: Recovering the Supernatural Worldview of the Bible* devotes a lot of space to a lot of weird passages. One of the strangest is Gen 6:1–4, the episode in the days of Noah where the "sons of God" (called the "Watchers" in Jewish literature written during the time between the Testaments) transgress the boundary between heaven and earth in an illicit relationship with the "daughters of humankind." The act produced the Nephilim, who are the forebears of the giant clans encountered by Moses and Joshua (Num 13:32–33).[1]

There have been many attempts to strip this passage of its supernatural elements in order to make it palatable to modern Bible students. Since this sort of material has been my academic focus for the past 15 years, I can tell you that all such attempts have significant flaws of exegesis and logical coherence. But the greatest flaw is that any view that humanizes the sons of God and denies the unusual nature of the Nephilim invariably violates the passage's original context and polemic meaning.

Any view that humanizes the sons of God and denies the unusual nature of the Nephilim invariably violates the passage's original context and polemic meaning.

Prior to 2010, that assertion may have been contestable. That is no longer the case. Recent scholarly work on

Mesopotamian literature associated with events before and after the great flood have produced clear, unambiguous, point-for-point parallels to what we read in Genesis 6:1–4. Those parallels demonstrate with no uncertainty that this biblical passage was specifically written to denigrate Mesopotamian ideas of the superiority of their gods and culture.

In the Mesopotamian material, the divine beings who lived at the time of the flood were called *apkallu*. They cohabited with human women, producing a new generation of *apkallu* who were not only divine-human hybrids, but also giants. Mesopotamian religion saw these generations of *apkallu* as great sages. Their survival via human women before the annihilation of the flood preserved pre-flood divine knowledge that had been taught to men. This knowledge was preserved in Babylon, which explained (to the Mesopotamian cultures) why their culture was superior to all others. Rather than deny the supernatural context of the Mesopotamian material, Genesis hits it head-on. The *apkallu* were not saviors. They were undeserving rivals to Yahweh of Israel and deserved to die. After the flood the giant *apkallu* became enemies of God's people, the Israelites. Whether we realize it or not, Gen 6:1–4 reports the first salvo in the long war against Yahweh and his people. This strange passage that modern readers keep at arm's length has hooks into other biblical passages, including the New Testament.

This new research comes from a thorough reexamination of the Sumerian and Akkadian flood epics. The insights were skillfully culled by cuneiform scholar Amar Annus in a 2010 journal article.[2] Annus' article is the most current study on the Mesopotamian *apkallu* available anywhere in any form. It supersedes all preceding work on this subject.[3] It deals a death blow to any nonsupernatural interpretation of Genesis 6:1–4.

What this means is that every commentary on Genesis you've come to trust can no longer be trusted on this passage because it was written before this new, ground-breaking research. They're like 8-track tapes—obsolete. The good news is that my book *The Unseen Realm* interacts with this new research at length. And there are a lot of issues like this one where I draw on recent research and provide a more up-to-date discussion than most commentaries. If you care about interpreting the Bible in its original context—including the supernatural worldview of the biblical writers—you should care about the latest insights from research on the ancient world.

13

What's in a Name?

"I am that I am"—God's response when Moses asks for his name is famous for both its simplicity and its mystery (Exod 3:14 LEB). What exactly does it mean?

In Hebrew, God says *ehyeh asher ehyeh* ("I am that I am"). The verb form for "I am" is *ehyeh*. If you've studied a language, you know that verbs—action words—have grammatical person and number. With most languages, "number" refers to singular or plural; "person" refers to the subject of the verb. When I taught biblical languages, I would explain it this way: *I* am number one (first person). *You* are second fiddle (second person). Everyone else (*he*, *she*, or *they*) is a third party (third person).

In this sentence, the name of God, *ehyeh*, is a first-person, singular form of the verb "to be" (*hayah*). It's a statement of self-existence—and, therefore, a *denial* of being created by any higher power or force.

> "I am that I am." God's response when Moses asks for his name is famous for both its simplicity and its mystery.

Yet, the consonants used in *ehyeh* are not exactly the same as those found in the name of God in thousands of other places in the Hebrew Old Testament: *y-h-w-h*. These four consonants are known as the sacred Tetragrammaton (meaning "four letters"). Out of reverence, Israelites didn't pronounce the name. In writing, they eventually provided the consonants with vowels for a different Hebrew word—*adonay* or "Lord."[1] English translations represent the sacred name with "Lᴏʀᴅ" in small capital letters. That actually isn't a translation of the four consonants, though. It's a reverential substitute for a word that was not spoken.

If *ehyeh* is the name God gives in Exodus 3:14, where does *yhwh* come from? For an answer, we need to take a closer look at the Hebrew's meaning and the forms it can take. *Ehyeh* and *yhwh* come from the same verb, *hayah* (meaning "to be"). *Ehyeh* is the first-person form of the verb and is typically translated as "I am." That same root word also appears as *hawah*, a standard spelling in texts older than the earliest manuscripts of the Hebrew Old Testament.[2] The name *yhwh* is the third-person form of *hawah*.

All this suggests that *yhwh* should be pronounced *yihweh*, which would mean "he is" (since it's in the third person). But that's problematic. Elsewhere in the Bible, the divine name is shortened to two consonants (*yh*; e.g., Exod 15:2), and Hebrew scribes always added an "a" vowel to it (*yah*). So if the first half of the name is *yah*, it wouldn't seem *yihweh* is the right option. That's why scholars prefer *yahweh* as the spelling of the divine name. But, as you might guess, that's disputed, too.

To unravel the debate over the mystery behind God's name, we have to dive deeper into the original language. Stick with me here—even if you don't know Hebrew, the possibilities present intriguing options for interpretation.

The most straightforward explanation is a technical one: *Yahweh* is a third-person form in what's called the imperfect conjugation of the Hiphil stem. It sounds complicated, but this conjugation basically accounts for the added "y" and the *yah* spelling of the shorter name. Since the Hiphil stem is used to indicate the subject's role as a *cause* for something else, the meaning of the divine name *yahweh* would be something like "he causes to be" or "he brings into existence." This would denote God as the one who is creator.

But here's the rub: There are no examples of this form of the verb *hayah/hawah* in *all* known ancient Hebrew writing samples *except* for the Old Testament. For that reason, some scholars don't like this explanation.[3] They want at least one parallel. For several linguistic reasons, they prefer to understand *y-h-w-h* simply as "he is" (*yihweh*) without regard to the shorter *yah* spelling.[4]

In the end, both possibilities are workable. One (*yihweh*) maintains the idea that God is uncreated; he just *is*. The other (*yahweh*) proposes that the God of Israel is the one who brings all things into being. He is and he is the creator. Both are powerful theological statements.

14

Lost at Sea

Israel's crossing of the Red Sea in Exod 14 has been spectacularly depicted several times for television and movies. But anyone who retraces the steps of Moses and the Israelites to discover where the crossing occurred finds a significant problem: The "Red Sea" in Israel's itinerary most likely *wasn't* what we think of as the Red Sea.

The problem originates with the biblical Hebrew phrase *yam suph*, usually rendered as "Red Sea" in English translations.[1] The phrase actually means "sea of reeds" or "reed sea." The word *yam* refers to a body of water which, of course, could include something as large as a sea. However, *suph* does not mean "red"; that word in Hebrew is *'adom* (used in Gen 25:30) or *'admoni* (used in Gen 25:25).

> *The "Red Sea" in Israel's itinerary most likely wasn't what we think of as the Red Sea.*

So the Israelites crossed "the sea of reeds," which refers to a body of water with reeds in it, most likely papyrus reeds. That description could not apply to the Red Sea since very few parts of the Red Sea are suitable for reeds to grow due to the salt content of the water. The phrase *yam suph* further complicates the identification of the crossing, since it is used in the Bible for watery locations in or near *both* prongs of the Red Sea. Some verses describe the eastern prong, the Gulf of Aqabah (1 Kgs 9:26; Exod 23:31; Num 21:4; Judg 11:16), but Num 33:8–10 describes the *yam suph* as being geographically oriented to the western prong of the Red Sea, the Gulf of Suez, a few days' journey from Egypt. This passage also has the Israelites passing "through the midst of the sea (*yam*)" before they ever get to the *yam suph* ("Red Sea"):

> And they set out from before Hahiroth and **passed through the midst of the sea** [*yam*] into the wilderness, and they went a three days' journey in the wilderness of Etham and camped at Marah. And they set out from Marah and came to Elim; at Elim there were twelve springs of water and seventy palm trees, and they camped there. And they set out from Elim and **camped by the Red Sea** (*yam suph*).[2]

It's possible that when the Israelites emerged from Egypt that they crossed a smaller body of water adjacent to the Red Sea—possibly one of the Bitter Lakes or Lake Timsah—rather than the Red Sea itself. But there's another option. Since biblical Hebrew words were originally written without vowels, the phrase *yam suph* could be read as *yam soph*. The odd-sounding result would be "the sea of the end" or "the sea of extinction"—a phrase that refers to an ancient cosmological notion that the world

---

Israelites who believed they were headed to the edge of the world—into the chaotic sea where none could survive—would have interpreted God's deliverance as an astonishing act of divine power.

---

was flat and surrounded by a water boundary. In this view, the Israelites would have thought they were approaching the end of the world, venturing out into the desert wilderness and straight into the primeval waters where no one could live.[3]

This view is mythic in tone, but it does not preclude a miraculous historical event. Israelites who believed they were headed to the edge of the world—into the chaotic sea where none could survive—would have interpreted God's deliverance as an astonishing act of divine power. To land safely on the other side of death's realm would be miraculous.

Although we can't determine the precise location of the crossing, the various possibilities in no way rule out God's providential intervention on behalf of His people.

15

The Slave before "Elohim"
in Exodus 21:1-6

Exodus 21:1-6 describes the potential situation in which a household slave desires to remain with his master rather than go free under the Israelite law mandating release each sabbatical (seventh) year.

> ¹ "Now these are the rules that you shall set before them. ² When you buy a Hebrew slave, he shall serve six years, and in the seventh he shall go out free, for nothing. ³ If he comes in single, he shall go out single; if he comes in married, then his wife shall go out with him. ⁴ If his master gives him a wife and she bears him sons or daughters, the wife and her children shall be her master's, and he shall go out alone. ⁵ But if the slave plainly says, 'I love my master, my wife, and my children; I will not go out free,' ⁶ then his master shall bring him to God [*elohim*], and he shall bring him to the door or the doorpost. And his master shall bore his ear through with an awl, and he shall be his slave forever.

The Hebrew word translated "God" in verse 6 is *elohim*. While *elohim* is plural in its formation, its meaning in the Old Testament is usually singular, and it frequently refers to the God of Israel. The simplest reading here is thus that *elohim* is singular and points to the God of Israel, and the two Israelites perform the brief ceremony "in the sight of God," so to speak, similar to a modern wedding in which the minister notes that everyone has been gathered "in the sight of God" to witness the couple's joining in marriage.

However, some argue that *elohim* here is plural in meaning as well in order to find scriptural warrant for the idea that Israel's elders and judges were present at the ceremony and thus that those men could have been called *elohim*. They then apply this proof text to Psalm 82, arguing that the *elohim* of Yahweh's council, mentioned in Ps 82:1, are really men, not divine beings. However, neither judges nor elders are found in Exod 21, and the Old Testament never uses the term *elohim* for human leaders anywhere else. Many presume that Exod 18 refers to the elders as *elohim*, but the text never makes that equation. *Elohim* there refers, as usual, to God. A comparison of Exod 21:1-6 with its parallel in Deut 15:12-18 further weakens this argument.

As noted above, *elohim* in Exod 21:6 could quite coherently refer to the singular "God"—but not to a group of humans. However, a comparison with Deut 15:12-18 raises the possibility that Exod 21:6 refers to a group of divine beings ("gods").

> [12] If your brother, a Hebrew man or a Hebrew woman, is sold to you, he shall serve you six years, and in the seventh year you shall let him go free from you.

[13] And when you let him go free from you, you shall not let him go empty-handed. [14] You shall furnish him liberally out of your flock, out of your threshing floor, and out of your winepress. As the Lord your God has blessed you, you shall give to him. [15] You shall remember that you were a slave in the land of Egypt, and the Lord your God redeemed you; therefore I command you this today. [16] But if he says to you, "I will not go out from you," because he loves you and your household, since he is well-off with you, [17] then you shall take an awl, and put it through his ear into the door, and he shall be your slave forever. And to your female slave you shall do the same. [18] It shall not seem hard to you when you let him go free from you, for at half the cost of a hired servant he has served you six years. So the Lord your God will bless you in all that you do.

The procedure in Exodus and Deuteronomy is the same, but the word *elohim* does not appear in Deuteronomy. If *elohim* referred to the God of Israel, there would be no logical reason for its removal from the law. (The same would be true if it referred to humans.) The only coherent rationale is that the writer (or a later editor) of Deuteronomy somehow knew that *elohim* referred to other divine beings ("gods" plural). Deuteronomy is famous for its strict monotheism (e.g., Deut 4:35, 39) and its commitment to the centralization of worship (Deut 12).

Deuteronomy is famous for its strict monotheism and its commitment to the centralization of worship.

The entire book, in fact, may have been written after the time of Moses, during or near the reign of Josiah, in the seventh century BC. Josiah is noted in Scripture for his great revival of Yahweh worship, which included the removal of idols and other religious objects that had caused the Israelites to worship other gods (2 Kgs 22–23). While arguing that the whole book of Deuteronomy is post-Mosaic and that it was written exclusively in the seventh century BC is extreme and problematic, it does seem plausible that scribes zealous to preserve Israel's monotheism could have been so concerned that Israelites might interpret *elohim* here as plural and thus entertain the idea of other gods that they simply removed the word. This seems unnecessary, even if the reference was plural, since the Old Testament assumes the existence of other gods (*elohim*) inferior to Yahweh (e.g., Deut 32:17; Ps 82:1). The scribe nevertheless took no chances.

One question remains: If the reference in Exod 21:6 is indeed plural, what "gods" does this Israelite law refer to? The most likely answer is *teraphim*, which were household figurines, likely of one's deceased ancestors. In Genesis 31, Rachel takes her father Laban's *teraphim* when fleeing Haran with Jacob (Gen 31:19, 34–45). David also apparently had *teraphim* in his house (1 Sam 19:13, 16). In fact, the authors of the Hebrew Bible (along with other ancient Near Eastern cultures) considered the disembodied human dead to be divine beings (see the use of *elohim* in 1 Sam 28:13), and *teraphim* represented those "gods" (*elohim*)—the family's ancestors. The existence of *teraphim* may point to ancestor worship, but it is unclear what would constitute worship. *Teraphim* may have served a similar purpose to modern remembrances of the dead today. Bereaved people leave flowers or other items of intimate connection at gravesides, presuming the dead are appreciative—that a connection between living and the dead remains. When others adorn their houses with photographs of deceased loved ones, it helps them remember them. The same can be said of *teraphim*. Leaving offerings at graves, or depositing them before *teraphim*, may simply have been the ancient Israelite equivalent of contemporary expressions of grief or respect.

Therefore, when a slave wanted to join the household out of love for his master, as in Exod 21, it would have been entirely appropriate for him to appear before the household's ancestors (*elohim*). Failure to do this would have, in fact, been deeply disrespectful to the dead. The editor of Deuteronomy, though, feared that the term would be misunderstood, so he had to update the law for the times.

16

The Angel of Yahweh in the Old Testament

The Angel of Yahweh (*mal'akh YHWH*) or the Angel of the LORD is an important figure in the Old Testament. This angel is not like other angels, since the essence of Yahweh dwells within him. Thus writers in the Old Testament often depict him as a surrogate Yahweh or even interchange the Angel with Yahweh himself. On at least one occasion, Yahweh and the Angel (the "second Yahweh") appear together in the same narrative scene. The Angel of Yahweh thus anticipates an Israelite belief in a Godhead—the view that God comprises more than one person, each of whom is identified as the presence of Yahweh. Jewish theologians prior to the New Testament era, observing these texts featuring the Angel and other "dual Yahweh" language, developed a theology of two Yahwehs (one visible, the other invisible spirit) or two powers in heaven. Jewish authorities declared this teaching a heresy after the second century AD.

The Angel as Yahweh

The account of the burning bush in Exod 3 is the most appropriate place to begin a discussion of the Angel of Yahweh:

And Moses was a shepherd with the flock of Jethro, his father-in-law, the priest of Midian, and he led the flock to the west *of* the desert, and he came to the mountain of **God** [*elohim*], to Horeb. ² And the **angel of Yahweh** [*mal'akh YHWH*] appeared to him in a flame of fire from the midst of a bush, and he looked, and there was the bush burning with fire, but the bush was not being consumed. ³ And Moses said, "Let me turn aside and see this great sight. Why does the bush not burn up?" ⁴ And **Yahweh** saw that he turned aside to see, and **God** [*elohim*] called to him from the midst of the bush, and he said, "Moses, Moses." And he said, "Here I *am*." ⁵ And he said, "You must not come near to here. Take off your sandals from on your feet, because the place on which you *are* standing, it *is* holy ground." ⁶ And he said, "I am the **God** [*elohim*] of your father, the **God** [*elohim*] of Abraham, the **God** [*elohim*] of Isaac, and the **God** [*elohim*] of Jacob." And Moses hid his face because he was afraid of looking at **God** [*elohim*]. (Exod 3:1–6 LEB)

God is not alone in the burning bush (compare Acts 7:30–35). According to the passage, the Angel and Yahweh are both clearly in the bush (Exod 3:2, 4). The Angel appears "out of the midst of a bush"; Yahweh calls to Moses "out of the bush." This passage illustrates the close identification and potential interchange between Yahweh and his Angel.

Although it is much less familiar than the burning bush episode, Exod 23:20–23 is the most crucial passage in the Old Testament for understanding the identity of the Angel of Yahweh:

Look, I *am about to* send an angel before you to guard you on the way and to bring you to the place that I have prepared. [21] Be attentive to him and listen to his voice; do not rebel against him, **because he will not forgive your transgression, for my name is in him.** [22] But if you listen attentively to his voice and do all that I say, I will be an enemy to your enemies and a foe to your foes. [23] When my angel goes before you and brings you to the Amorites and the Hittites and the Perizzites and the Canaanites and the Hivites and the Jebusites, I will wipe them out. (LEB)

This Angel has the authority to pardon or withhold pardon for sins, something only God can do. God also gives the Angel responsibility for bringing the Israelites to the Promised Land—something for which the Angel later takes credit (Judg 2:1–3; compare Josh 5:13–15), though God himself also takes the same credit elsewhere (Josh 24:6–8; Jer 2:7; Amos 2:10). The Angel's authority and interchangeability with Yahweh as Israel's leader derive from the fact that Yahweh's "name is in him" (Exod 23:21).

Exodus 23:20–23 is the most crucial passage in the Old Testament for understanding the identity of the Angel of Yahweh.

The "name" of Yahweh does not merely refer to the four consonants of God's preferred name for himself, YHWH (called the Tetragrammaton). Rather, it refers to Yahweh himself. Old Testament writers at times refer to God himself as "the Name," a practice still used by modern orthodox Jews. To avoid pronouncing the sacred consonants, these Jews substitute YHWH with the Hebrew *ha-shem* ("the Name"). Old Testament writers, in fact, use the same sort of substitution, at times even portraying "the Name" as a person or man (Isa 30:27–28; Ps 20:1, 7). That Yahweh can bring deliverance is a familiar idea, but four consonants do not protect the people of God—God himself protects them.

The book of Deuteronomy provides some helpful explanation to the "Name theology" of the Old Testament. Deuteronomy frequently refers to Israel's worship of God at the place where Yahweh will "put his name" (Deut 12:4, 21) or "make his name dwell" (Deut 12:11; 14:23; 16:2, 6, 11). According to these descriptions, there will come a day that Israel will not have a temple with YHWH inscribed on the door. Rather, Yahweh's Name is his very presence or essence, and Yahweh himself will dwell in that temple (see 1 Kings 8).

> *Yahweh's name is his very presence or essence.*

These passages provide the necessary context for Exod 23:20–23. Yahweh himself dwells in the Angel of Yahweh. In effect, the Angel *is* Yahweh embodied in human form (compare Josh 5:13–15). Recalling that, according to Exod 23:23, the Angel of Yahweh brings Israel to the Promised Land and defeats its inhabitants, Deut 4:37–38 take on a new light:

> And because he loved your ancestors he chose their descendants after them. And he brought you forth from Egypt **with his own presence**, by his great strength, [38] to drive out nations greater and more numerous than you from before you, to bring you *and* to give to you their land *as* an inheritance, as *it is* this day. (LEB)

This passage, taken with Exod 23 and others in which God himself brings Israel into the land, reveals that the Angel of Yahweh, Yahweh himself, and the "presence" of God are synonymous. The Angel is Yahweh because Yahweh is inseparable from his presence.

This identification between Yahweh and the Angel provides a theological context for other passages in the Old Testament. For example, in Gen 31:11–13, the Angel of God (*mal'akh ha'elohim*), alluding to Yahweh's earlier appearance to Jacob after he had left his home, tells Jacob in a dream, "I am the God of Bethel." Jacob, just prior to his dramatic encounter with Esau on his journey home, encounters a "man" who accosts him; according to Hos 12:3–5, Jacob struggled with *elohim* ("God"). This divine man changes Jacob's name to Israel, signifying that God has been with him, as promised so many years earlier. Later, in Gen 48, when Jacob is near death and pronouncing blessing on Joseph's sons, he recalls this event in a way that highlights the fusion of Yahweh and the Angel:

> And he blessed Joseph and said, "The **God** [*ha-elohim*] before whom my fathers, Abraham and Isaac, walked, the **God** [*ha-elohim*] who shepherded me all my life unto this day, the **angel** [*ha-mal'ak*] who redeemed me from all evil, may **he** bless the boys." (Gen 48:15–16a LEB)

The Bible very clearly teaches that, on the one hand, God is eternal and existed before all things and, on the other, that angels are created beings. The explicit parallel of "God" and "Angel," therefore, certainly does not imply that God is an angel. Rather, it affirms that *this* Angel *is* God. The verb "bless," moreover, is grammatically *singular*; a grammatically plural verb would indicate that Jacob is asking two different persons to bless the boys—the singular thus indicates a fusion of the two divine beings.

The Angel and Yahweh in Simultaneous Appearance

Judges 6 records Gideon's call to serve as a judge in Israel. In this call, Gideon encounters *both* the Angel of Yahweh and the voice of Yahweh—just as Moses had:[1]

[12] The **angel of Yahweh appeared to him [Gideon] and said to him**, "Yahweh is with you, you mighty warrior."

[13] Gideon said to him, "Excuse me, my lord. If Yahweh is with us, why then has all this happened to us? Where are all his wonderful deeds that our ancestors recounted to us, saying, 'Did not Yahweh bring us up from Egypt?' But now Yahweh has forsaken us; he has given us into the palm of Midian."

[14] **And Yahweh turned to him and said**, "Go in this your strength, and you will deliver Israel from the palm of Midian. Did I not send you?"

[15] He [Gideon] said to him, "Excuse me, my lord. How will I deliver Israel? Look, my clan is the weakest in Manasseh, and I am the youngest in my father's house."

[16] **And Yahweh said to him**, "But I will be with you, and you will defeat Midian as if they are one man."

[17] And he [Gideon] said to him, "Please, if I have found favor in your eyes, show me a sign that you

are speaking with me. [18] Please, do not depart from here until I come back to you and bring out my gift and set it out before you."

And he [the angel] said, "I will stay until you return." ...

[21] Then **the angel of Yahweh** reached out the tip of the staff that was in his hand, and he touched the meat and the unleavened cakes; and fire went up from the rock and consumed the meat and the unleavened cakes. **And the angel of Yahweh went from his sight.**

[22] And Gideon realized that he was the angel of Yahweh; and Gideon said, "Oh, my lord Yahweh! For now I have seen the angel of Yahweh face to face."

[23] **And Yahweh said to him**, "Peace be with you. Do not fear; you will not die."

In this passage, the Angel vanishes in verse 21, but Yahweh is still talking to Gideon in verse 23. The Angel both *is* and *is not* Yahweh. This sort of description parallels New Testament passages about Jesus, who is God but is also not the Father.

Jesus, the Angel, and the Name

Several New Testament passages subtly identify Jesus with the Angel of Yahweh. For example, Jude 5 reads:

Now I want to remind you, *although* you know everything once and for all, that Jesus, having saved the people out of the land of Egypt, the second time destroyed those who did not believe. (LEB)

In this short verse, Jude credits Jesus with delivering the Israelites from Egypt and destroying Israel's enemies. This passage refers to Exod 23:20–23, where the Angel of Yahweh, in whom is the Name, leads Israel out of Egypt. Although some manuscripts of the New Testament do not read "Jesus" here, the reading is most likely original.[2]

In John 17:1–26, while in prayer awaiting Judas's betrayal, Jesus describes himself several times as one who was given the name of the Father and who manifests the name to the people of God (LEB):

> **I have revealed your name** to the men whom you gave me out of the world. They were yours, and you have given them to me, and they have kept your word. (17:6)

> Holy Father, **keep them in your name, which you have given to me**, so that they may be one, just as we *are*. When I was with them, **I kept them in your name, which you have given to me.** (17:11b–12a)

> And I do not ask on behalf of these only, but also on behalf of those who believe in me through their word, that they all may be one, **just as you, Father, *are* in me** and I *am* in you. (17:20–21a)

> **And I made known to them your name**, and will make *it* known, in order that the love *with* which you loved me may be in them, and I *may be* in them. (17:26)

Jesus here states both that he has been given the "name" of the Father (17:11) and that the Father is "in" him (17:21). The language would seem odd without the Old Testament background discussed above where the "Name" represents the essence of Yahweh himself. The Name—the very presence of Yahweh—was "in" the Angel of Yahweh, implying that the Angel was the embodied presence of Yahweh. John elsewhere calls Jesus the "Word," language that draws on several Old Testament passages that allude to Yahweh's earthly presence as the "word" (Gen 15:1; 1 Sam 3:21). Here John casts Jesus as the embodied Name, who, as the incarnate Yahweh, came to reveal that Name, God himself, to humanity. Jesus, in other words, did not teach anyone God's name; they knew the name already from the Old Testament. Rather, he was God come to humankind.

> *John casts Jesus as the embodied Name, who, as the incarnate Yahweh, came to reveal that Name, God himself, to humanity.*

In the same manner that Old Testament authors use "the Name" as a substitute reference for Yahweh, other New Testament writers use the "the Name" as a substitution for Jesus:

> And they summoned the apostles, beat *them*, commanded *them* not to speak in the name of Jesus, and released *them*. [41] So they went out from the presence of the Sanhedrin rejoicing, because they had been considered worthy to be dishonored for the sake of **the name**. [42] Every day, both in the temple *courts* and from house *to house*, they did not stop teaching and

proclaiming the good news *that* the Christ *was* Jesus.
(Acts 5:40–42 LEB)

The expression here indicates, at the very least, a similar mode of thinking as in the Old Testament—that these Jews can refer to the God they follow with the phrase "the Name," their ethnic status giving the phrase a distinct Old Testament flavor. Moreover, it is clear that the Name for whom the apostles suffer is Jesus. In Romans 10, Paul says:

That if you confess with your mouth "Jesus *is* Lord" and believe in your heart that God raised him from the dead, you will be saved. … For "**everyone who calls upon the name of the Lord** will be saved." (Rom 10:9, 13 LEB)

The quotation in verse 13 comes from Joel 2:32, which reads, "everyone who calls on the name of Yahweh will be rescued" (LEB). The apostle Paul here, as he does many times throughout his writings, deftly links the confession of Jesus as Lord in verse 9 with the statement of the Old Testament prophet. Since "the Name" and Yahweh were interchangeable in Israelite theology, trusting in "the Name of Yahweh" meant trusting in Yahweh. Likewise, trusting in the name of the Lord, who of course is Yahweh in the Old Testament quotation, is the same as confessing Jesus as Lord.

17

Salvation in Old Testament Israel

The New Testament's rejection of earning God's favor by works and its emphasis on salvation by grace through faith (e.g., Eph 2:8–9; Gal 2:16; Rom 4:1–12) has led many people to presume that the Old Testament teaches that people could merit salvation by obeying the Mosaic law. However, this is not the case.

Old Testament theology, with its complex sacrificial system, had a firm grasp of the problem of sin, which was variously defined as being ritually impure or transgressing God's moral law. As members of a stable nation trying to walk with their God, literally not a day could pass in the normal course of Israel's life when they were not reminded that they were imperfect and impure in the sight of a holy God. Nothing would create the idea that human goodness could earn God's pleasure. However, since living according to God's law and maintaining the purity of sacrificial worship required great human effort, Israelites also knew that salvation was not a purely passive status. The issue is not that human effort was not part of salvation. It would have been foreign to the Israelite to think that faith was not a fundamental requirement for salvation or that an individual's own works resulted in God owing salvation to anyone.

It would have been foreign to the Israelite to think that faith was not a fundamental requirement for salvation or that an individual's own works resulted in God owing salvation to anyone.

Therefore, in its framing, Old Testament salvation was the same as New Testament salvation. In the New Testament, works were essential to salvation (Jas 2:14–26), but they were never the *meritorious cause* of salvation; God owed salvation to no one on the basis of works. This is not contrary to Paul's assertion that no one was justified by works. James and Paul could thus be fused this way: "For by grace are you saved through faith, which without works is dead" (Eph 2:8; Jas 2:17). No element can be eliminated. Jesus said that a tree (and hence a believer) was known by its fruit (Matt 12:33). If an individual does not have works ("fruit"), there is no evidence of salvation. The presence of works is essential for calling someone a believer. But works do not put God in the position of owing salvation. Salvation comes by faith in Christ (its object), which produces works. Both must be present. Old Testament salvation can be framed the same way, though the object of faith differs.

With respect to the Old Testament Israelite, faith was essential to standing in right relationship to God. The Israelite had to believe that Yahweh, the God of Israel, was the true God, superior to all other gods. This would produce fruit in the form of loyal worship of only Yahweh and no other god. Old Testament Israelites also had to believe that Yahweh had come to their forefathers—Abraham, Isaac, and Jacob—and made a covenant with them that made them his exclusive people. This covenant included specific promises to be believed by faith. Faith in the divine origin of the covenant and its promises involved obedience. The language of the Abrahamic covenant (Gen 12:1–3; 15:1–6) was frequently repeated in connection with obedience to God (e.g., Gen 17:1–6; 22:18; 26:5). The patriarchs could not have disobeyed God's commands by rejecting circumcision, refusing to go where God commanded, and rejecting sacrifice, and still received God's blessing. The children of the patriarchs also had to believe that the God who delivered them from Egypt was the same God of their forefathers. That same God gave Israel the law to distinguish them as his unique possession of humanity on earth (e.g., Exod 20–23; Lev 10–11). An Israelite who believed he was a child of the God of Sinai produced fruit by obeying the law. The law of Sinai was connected to the promises given to Abraham (Lev 26). Faith in Yahweh and loyalty to Yahweh were both part of salvation (right relationship to God) in the Old Testament. Individuals could not be rightly-related to God by means of only one.

In all this, Israelites could not do the works of the law and then presume God owed them salvation. God was in relationship with Israel because he chose to be in that relationship—he chose this before obedience was any issue. God extended grace by calling Abraham; Abraham believed, and then Abraham showed that belief by obedience (Rom 4). The concept "circumcision of the heart" is telling in regard to the balance of faith and works. Circumcision was the sign of the covenant. Since performing it required human activity, it could be thought of as a good work. God desired obedience—the submission of one's will—on this matter. "Circumcision of the heart" speaks of a heart that believes, not a work. It is a heart submitted to God, not merely the will. A circumcised heart was a believing heart, and it was essential for right relationship to God (Deut 10:16; 30:6; Jer 4:4; 31:33; 32:39, 40; Ezek 11:19; 36:26, 27).

In the Old Testament law and the sacrificial system, failure was inevitable; fellowship with God would inevitably be broken. Moreover, humans were impure by nature and unable to approach the perfect divine presence. The book of Leviticus indicates that people could purge ("atone for") the impurity caused by sin and transgression through sacrifice, which resulted in forgiveness (Lev 4:20, 26, 31, 35; 5:10, 13, 16, 18; 6:7; Num 15:25–28). But they did not *earn* forgiveness; God provided the entire means of forgiveness—the sacrificial system—through his grace. God was not forced to provide a means of atonement or reveal what he would accept for atonement. The means of restoring fellowship with God was an extension of God's grace.

18

Where the Wild (Demonic) Things Are

Students of the cultural context of the Bible are familiar with the association between animals and idolatry. The idolatrous worship of the golden calf (*egel*; Exod 32:1-24) makes the connection explicit. Even after the Israelites entered into a covenant relationship with Yahweh at Sinai, Moses and Aaron had to act to prevent the people from sacrificing to "goat demons" (*se'irim*) in the wilderness (Lev 17:7). Centuries later, the apostasy of King Jeroboam returned this idolatry to the northern kingdom of Israel ("He appointed his own priests for the high places and for the goat idols [*se'irim*] and for the calves [*agalim*] that he had made"; 2 Chr 11:15).

The link between the demonic and the desert has strong Old Testament precedent.

The reference to "goat demons" (*se'irim*) in the wilderness and their idols is of special interest because the link between the demonic and the desert has strong Old Testament precedent. The connection would have been apparent to Israelites because a range of wild animals and birds were specifically associated with foreign gods and their idols in pagan religions of biblical times. For example, consider the listing of desert creatures in Isaiah 34:

> But the hawk and the porcupine shall possess it, the owl [*yanshoph*] and the raven shall dwell in it. ... Thorns shall grow over its strongholds, nettles and thistles in its fortresses. It shall be the haunt of jackals [*tannim*], an abode for ostriches. And wild animals [*tsiyyim*] shall meet with hyenas [*iyyim*]; the wild goat [*se'irim*] shall cry to his fellow; indeed, there the night bird [*lilith*] settles and finds for herself a resting place. (Isa 34:11, 13–14)

The Hebrew terms in this passage are associated with false gods in the religions of the ancient Near East.[1] The *yanshoph* of verse 11 has been identified with the ibis, the animal emblem of the god Thoth, worshiped by ancient Egyptians.

The words *tannim* and *iyyim* (vv. 13–14) are set in parallel relationship elsewhere in Isaiah (13:22), possibly suggesting the terms were synonyms for a wild dog.[2] However, the Septuagint (the Greek translation of the Old Testament), renders both words with *onokentauros*, variously interpreted as "hairless ape"[3] or "donkey-centaur, mythic creature."[4] Since *tsiyyim* is related to vocabulary for arid places, the term is considered to point to a sinister "desert creature." Its placement in Isaiah 34:14, in parallel with the "goat demons" (*se'irim*), strongly implies a demonic meaning.[5] This notion is strengthened by the reference in the same verse to *lilith*, a female demon with a long history stretching back to Sumerian material.[6] She was considered a night-demon who took the lives of small children and seduced men nocturnally.

By New Testament times, the association of demons and the wilderness would have been very familiar to most Jews. Demonic encounters in the Gospels are often set in the desert (e.g., Matt 12:43-45; Luke 8:29; 11:24-26), and Jesus encountered Satan in the wilderness (Matt 4:1-11).

This last encounter is telling, for the Son of God dispatches the desert's most lethal threat with three citations from Deuteronomy (6:13, 16; 8:3)—a text famously set in Israel's desert encampment just before the conquest of Canaan. Jewish readers of the Gospel accounts would not have missed the point: Jesus of Nazareth has overcome the powers of darkness; believe in him.

19

The Secret Things
Belong to the Lord

We're all guilty of giving excuses. Although we know deep down that excuses don't solve problems, that doesn't stop us from using them to deflect attention away from our mistakes and flaws. Sometimes we even use Scripture as an excuse to avoid addressing difficult Bible passages. We might appeal to Deuteronomy 29:29 when we encounter biblical passages that seem too confusing or weird: "The secret things belong to the Lord our God."

Bible students, teachers, and professors alike often cite this verse to avoid researching problematic or strange passages. It can serve as a way of expressing our real excuses in a more "spiritual" way:

> "I want my Bible to be simple—you're making my head hurt."

> "This isn't important. Analyzing the Bible doesn't help us love Jesus."

> "This is stuff only pastors need to know; let's be more practical."

The problem is this verse doesn't mean what its advocates think it means. There's no Bible verse that discourages us from studying the Bible. The misuse of Deuteronomy 29:29 stems from our tendency to focus on just the first half of the verse. The complete verse provides a contextual clue for what's really in view:

> The secret things belong to the LORD our God, but the things that are revealed belong to us and to our children forever, that we may do all the words of this law.

The key phrase here is "this law." Deuteronomy 29:29 is the climax of Moses' lengthy sermon about receiving God's blessings for obedience to his laws or curses for disobedience upon entering the promised land.

Moses' sermon begins in Deuteronomy 27. The first eight verses outline the ceremonial duties the Israelites had to perform upon entering Canaan: They were to affirm "all the words of this law"—referring to Deuteronomy 5–26, which contains laws that repeat and amplify those God had given to the nation 40 years earlier at Sinai (Deut 27:3). Upon entering the promised land, the Israelites were to ritually enact a ceremony reaffirming their commitment to God's laws (Deut 27:9–14). The rest of chapter 27 and the entirety of chapter 28 detail how disobedience to God's laws would result in the people and the land being accursed; conversely, obedience would produce overflowing blessing. Deuteronomy 29 then reviews Israel's

There's no Bible verse that discourages us from studying the Bible.

history of failure amid God's covenantal faithfulness. The history lesson comes to a close with Deuteronomy 29:29.

Reading this verse fully and in context reveals that it isn't granting us permission to skip things that are difficult to understand or to avoid analyzing God's word. It's a warning: Concealed acts of sin—transgressions of the laws listed in Moses' sermon—are known to God. While the Israelites were responsible for dealing with known violations of God's law, secret transgressions would be dealt with by God, who knows all things. Recognizing Deuteronomy 29:29 for what it really is may result in more effort in our Bible studies, but more important, taking its lesson to heart will build spiritual character.

20

The Ongoing Battle of Jericho

The spectacular fall of Jericho's walls in Joshua 6 ranks as one of the most memorable stories in the Old Testament. It stands alongside epic tales like the parting of the Red Sea and the battle between David and Goliath. But many consider the description of events in the book of Joshua a litmus test for the Bible's historical fallibility.

The modern debate over Jericho's historicity has raged for decades. It's a complex battleground with strategic assaults from multiple perspectives. Archaeology and chronology are on the controversy's frontlines.

The Biblical Account

To understand the conflict, we need a clear picture of the chronology of events as recorded in the Bible. Following the exodus from Egypt, Joshua replaced Moses as Israel's leader (Num 27:18-23; Deut 31:7-8). He led the conquest of Jericho. According to 1 Kings 6:1, the fourth year of King Solomon's reign marked 480 years since the exodus. Solomon's fourth year is commonly dated to 966 BC, which places the exodus in 1446 BC (known as the "early" date).[1] Israel would have arrived at Sinai a few months later. According to the Pentateuch, they spent 13 months there before venturing to the promised land, where their spiritual failures prompted God to sentence them to wandering the desert for forty years (Num 10:11; 14:26–33). About forty years later Israel once again prepared to enter the land under Joshua (Deut 2:14). This literal reading of the chronology, particularly 1 Kings 6:1, places the fall of Jericho around 1400 BC.

The Archaeological View

Since the mid-20th century, many archaeologists who focus on the biblical world have argued that it is impossible to reconcile the timeline of the biblical account with archaeological data. They argue that (1) Jericho was destroyed in 1250 BC, but the city had no walls; (2) there was no walled city in 1400 BC when the book of Joshua reports Jericho's walls falling—in fact the city was unoccupied; and (3) there is little evidence of a broader Israelite conquest of Canaan in 1250 BC.[2]

These archaeologists claim the evidence for Jericho's fall points to a date nearly 200 years later—around 1250 BC, near the end of the Late Bronze Age (1550–1200 BC). Archaeological work on Jericho has shown that the city was uninhabited from 1550 BC to about 1300 BC. Furthermore, the archaeological record shows the city had no walls, which contradicts (and, they argue, *corrects*) archaeological work conducted in the early 20th century that revealed burned walls dating to around 1400 BC (see Josh 7:24). However, later research re-dated those walls much *earlier* than where the literal chronology of the Bible places the destruction of Jericho. Furthermore, the archaeological record of other cities allegedly conquered by Joshua shows no sign of destruction.[3]

The View from Another Bunker

Yet, other evidence mars this argument. Pottery from Jericho dating to around 1400 BC, apparently ignored or unrecognized by some archaeologists, does indeed exist. The same can be said for city walls, specifically walls that had *collapsed*, not broken down into the city. Egyptian scarabs found in Jericho cemeteries, etched with names of pharaohs who reigned from the 1700s through the 1300s BC, contradict the claim that the city was unoccupied in 1400 BC. The level of the city (Jericho IV) corresponding to the 1400 BC date shows evidence of sudden siege. The biblical account says Joshua's attack took place in early spring, after the harvest (Josh 2:6; 3:15; 4:9; 5:10). Several large storage jars still full of harvested food were found among the ruins in level IV.[4]

Furthermore, the conquest account in Joshua does not say that *all* the cities taken by Israel were destroyed or burned. In many instances, the account merely says the inhabitants were "driven out" and the cities occupied by Israelites. This would explain the lack of evidence of Canaanite cities being destroyed. Consequently, some archaeologists still argue for the integrity of the biblical account according to the literal chronological reading that renders the early (1446 BC) date for the exodus and a 1400 BC conquest.

> *It's important to remember that, while the battle over Jericho still rages, it's not a death match for biblical inerrancy.*

The Figurative View

Some biblical scholars present a third option. They lobby for the accuracy of the Joshua account but are content to go with the 1250 BC date held by most archaeologists—arguing that the archaeological record is consistent with military campaigns described in Joshua since the book describes the destruction of only particular sites.[5] In this view, the 480 years of 1 Kings 6:1—which supplies a chronology for the exodus—is taken as a figurative number, not a literal one. The 480 years described in this passage are divisible by 40 (12 x 40). The number 40 occurs more than 100 times in the Old Testament. The reigns of many judges and kings seem to be 40 years, and so scholars suspect that the number is a deliberate marker for a generation or transition (e.g., Judg 3:11, 31; 8:28; 1 Sam 4:18; 2 Sam 2:10; 5:4; 1 Kgs 2:11; 11:42). As a result, the dates of the exodus and conquest may be flexible.

It's important to remember that, while the battle over Jericho still rages, it's not a death match for biblical inerrancy.

21

Scripture's Sacred Trees

Before his death, Joshua gathered all of Israel to Shechem to deliver his final words (Josh 24). He demanded that everyone within the sound of his voice "choose this day whom you will serve" (24:15)—the God of their fathers or the foreign gods of their enemies. The choice was obvious for Joshua, and that's pretty much where the story ends for many. Yet, something intriguing happens after Joshua's statement of faith:

> And the people said to Joshua, "The LORD our God we will serve, and his voice we will obey." So Joshua made a covenant with the people that day, and put in place statutes and rules for them at Shechem. And Joshua wrote these words in the Book of the Law of God. And he took a large stone and set it up there under the terebinth that was by the sanctuary of the LORD. (24:24-26)

This passage tells us that Joshua wrote down the covenant promise vowed that day and then put a big rock underneath a tree to remind people of the event. An Israelite witness would definitely know that their words had been added to "the Book of the Law of God." The custom of erecting a commemorative stela—a large stone with a flat surface for writing—was a common event. Hundreds of these stones have survived from the ancient Near East. But equally as important to an Israelite—and often overlooked by us—was the terebinth.

A terebinth was a tree, but it was no ordinary tree. This was the tree that stood "by the sanctuary of the LORD" (24:26). Why would the Israelites put their sanctuary—the tabernacle structure with the ark of the covenant—next to a tree? Why even mention the tree?

In the Old Testament, trees often marked sacred sites—places of divine encounter. This particular tree marked a divine encounter at the core of Israel's existence. Genesis 12:6–7 records that Yahweh appeared to Abram at Shechem at the oak of Mamre, where Yahweh makes the promises of the covenant.[1] Here, Yahweh chooses Abraham and says that his offspring would be a great nation through whom all the nations would be blessed. Later Jacob buries his family's idols at this same spot to fulfill a vow to Yahweh (Gen 35:4). Jacob's act is no coincidence. His gesture recalls the incident that birthed Israel's covenant relationship. The oak at Shechem became a sacred site.

In the Old Testament, trees often marked sacred sites—places of divine encounter.

These events explain why the tree at Shechem was special for Joshua and the Israelites—it marked holy ground. Later, in Judges 9:5–6, Gideon's son Abimelech was declared king "by the oak of the pillar at Shechem." The "pillar" is a possible reference to the stela erected by Joshua before his death. This pillar appears again in Judges 9, where it is associated with divine revelation (Judg 9:34-37).

The Old Testament contains many other allusions to sacred trees and "tree language." The tree of life in Eden (Gen 2:9) is quite obviously associated with the presence of God. In Judges 4:4-5 the prophetess Deborah customarily sat under "the palm tree of Deborah" to fulfill her ministry and receive revelation from God (compare 1 Kgs 13:14).

And then there is the most sacred tree in Scripture—the cross, the place of our own divine encounter. Paul, speaking of Jesus, reminds us that "cursed is everyone who is hanged on a tree" (Gal 3:13). Jesus bore that curse for us so that we could be part of God's holy family. But the poignant irony is that Jesus was the embodied Word of the LORD who had once appeared to Abram (Gen 12:6-7; 15:1) promising he would be the father of a holy nation.[2] Jesus' work on the cross—his work of salvation on our behalf—fulfilled the covenant promised at the tree of Shechem.

22

Boaz—the Lawbreaker?

The book of Ruth contains one of the happy-ending stories of the Old Testament: Ruth, a destitute widow, marries Boaz, "a worthy man," and in doing so, saves her grieving mother-in-law from a life of certain poverty. But what readers may not realize is that by marrying Ruth, Boaz appears to have violated an Old Testament law: "No Ammonite or Moabite may enter the assembly of the LORD. Even to the tenth generation, none of them may enter the assembly of the LORD forever" (Deut 23:3).

The book of Ruth leaves no ambiguity about Ruth's heritage and situation. She was a Moabite (Ruth 1:4) who had married Mahlon, an Israelite man living in Moab with his family to escape famine in his hometown of Bethlehem (4:10). We know the rest of the story—how Mahlon, along with his brother and father, died (1:3–5); how Ruth journeyed to Bethlehem with her grieving and impoverished mother-in-law Naomi (1:6–19); how Boaz honored the law of the levirate (Deut 25:5–10) and redeemed Ruth through marriage, preserving Mahlon's name and Elimelech's property on Naomi's behalf (Ruth 4:9–10). But when she married Boaz, did Ruth not "enter the assembly of the LORD"?

Is this heartwarming story just a flagrant transgression of Old Testament law?

The question becomes more uncomfortable when we realize that, later in Israel's history, both Nehemiah and Ezra criticized the men of Israel for marrying foreign women after the return from exile (Neh 13:23-27; Ezra 10). Ezra actually sanctioned the marriages' termination, even if they had produced children (Ezra 10:10-19, 44). Nehemiah mentions that some of these unions were with women from Moab (Neh 13:23).

Some scholars try to absolve Boaz by focusing on ways to interpret the phrase "the assembly of the LORD" in Deuteronomy 23:3. The noun translated "assembly" (*qahal*) refers broadly to a gathering or group. In certain passages it clearly refers to all the Israelites collectively as a nation (Exod 16:3; Lev 16:17). Other times it refers to an assembly of only Israelite men (Judg 21:5, 8; Josh 8:35) or a governing body responsible for public business and judicial decisions (1 Kgs 12:3; Jer 26:16-17; Ezek 23:45-47). Some have suggested that Boaz could marry Ruth because the prohibition refers only to the leadership of Israel. Yet it's difficult to demonstrate that this instance wasn't speaking of the entire community when the phrase does elsewhere.

> *By marrying Ruth, Boaz appears to have violated an Old Testament law.*

Instead, let's compare Deuteronomy 23:3 (and hence Boaz's marriage) with other Old Testament perspectives on foreigners living in Israel. Several passages distinguish foreigners from the collective assembly of Israelites (Num 15:15, 26; 2 Chr 30:25). Foreigners did not have equal status under all Old Testament laws—they were excluded from laws restricting indentured servitude (Lev 25:39-43, 46, 54-55), debt release (Deut 15:2-3), and loaning money at interest (Deut 23:19-20). And while intermarriage with foreign women was generally forbidden, there were exceptions (Deut 21:10-14). The case of Rahab is perhaps most telling: She had clearly converted to belief in Yahweh (Josh 2:11-12; Jas 2:25) and was allowed to live in Israel (Josh 6:25).

This is crucial: A foreigner had come to embrace Yahweh—the LORD—as the true God. Ezra and Nehemiah's accounts make no mention of conversions. But in the case of Boaz's redemption of Ruth, her allegiance to the God of Israel is front and center: "Your people shall be my people, and your God my God" (Ruth 1:16).[1] Boaz had not sinned by marrying a Moabite because Ruth's loyalties were clearly with Yahweh, the God of Israel.

23

Of Mice and Manhood

Bible readers are familiar with the Israelites' shocking loss of the ark of the covenant into the hands of the Philistines (1 Sam 4:11–22). Adding insult to injury, the Philistines took the ark to Ashdod and placed it in the temple of their god, Dagon (5:1–2). Yahweh's response—reducing the idol of Dagon to a grotesque stump without limbs—was swift and dramatic (5:3–5). But God was not content with this vivid display of contempt for Dagon. The people of Ashdod had to be taught a lesson—one just as unforgettable.

First Samuel 5:6 tells us that God punished the Philistines with a bodily affliction called *ophalim* in Hebrew, often translated "tumors" and thought to refer to hemorrhoids.[1] "Tumors" is actually not a translation of the term that appears in the traditional text of the Hebrew Bible, the Masoretic text. Rather, it is a translation of a different word suggested by ancient scribes in what's known as a *Kethiv-Qere* reading—a note placed in the margin of Hebrew manuscripts by Masoretic scribes. *Kethiv* means "what is written" in the Hebrew text (in this case, *ophalim*) and *Qere* means "what should be read." Scribes substituted the word *tehorim* ("swellings") in 1 Samuel 5–6 for *ophalim*.[2]

This scribal change is odd since *ophel* (the singular form of *ophalim*) simply means "hill, bulge" (Mic 4:8; Isa 32:14).[3]

Aside from this manuscript issue, the term is puzzling because the regretful Philistines sent *ophalim* of gold and five golden mice as a guilt offering to Yahweh when they released the ark (1 Sam 6:4–18). The sets of five corresponded to the five cities of the Philistines (6:17). Since the god Dagon (outside Mesopotamia) was associated with grain and harvest, the reference to mice "that ravage the land" points to a decimation of Philistine crops (6:5). In turn, many interpreters justify adopting the scribal suggestion of tumors by arguing that the reference to mice might indicate bubonic plague. But how would one fashion a "tumor" of gold?

The Philistines were rightly terrified. Yahweh, the God of Israel, made it clear that he had complete power over their immediate and future survival as a people.

Recent archaeological discoveries have produced an alternative possibility—an affliction that would strike terror into any ancient culture that also served to mock Dagon and Philistine religion.[4] In the 1990s, archaeologists working at Ashkelon (one of the five Philistine cities named in this episode) discovered seven bronze vessels in the form of the male phallus. Typically such objects were used in rituals dealing with fertility (of both the human population and the land). These objects are well-known in the Aegean, the area from which most scholars believe the Philistines originated. This raises the possibility that the objects fashioned by the Philistines were these types of phallic objects.

It is quite understandable that *ophel* ("mound, bulge") could be used to refer to such objects euphemistically.

What is the theological takeaway? Yahweh may have afflicted the Philistines by eliminating their food supply and sending some sort of disease that prevented copulation—and thus, having children. The Philistines were rightly terrified. Yahweh, the God of Israel, made it clear that he had complete power over their immediate and future survival as a people. Their release of the ark was literally a choice between life and death.

24

Samuel's Ghost and Saul's Judgment

The afterlife is one of biblical theology's most compelling themes. Death is not final; there is life beyond the grave. We associate this idea with our final fate. But the Bible has a wider perspective—one that includes what we would commonly think of as ghosts. First Samuel 28 is one of the clearest windows into the world of the living dead.

Having expelled all the mediums from Israel, Saul nevertheless commands his servants to find a medium after God refuses to offer him guidance against the Philistines (1 Sam 28:3–7). Saul visits the medium at Endor by night and asks her to contact the deceased Samuel (28:8–11). She complies and, upon seeing Samuel, panics, believing that Saul has tricked her to expose her illicit practices. Here's where the story takes a spooky turn. Saul asks the medium, "What do you see?" She replies, "I see a god coming up out of the earth. ... An old man is coming up, and he is wrapped in a robe" (28:13–14).

Saul immediately discerns that it is Samuel ascending from the underworld realm of the dead. There is no indication in the biblical text that the medium is lying or that she is deceived. When Samuel asks Saul, "Why have you disturbed me by bringing me up?" the distraught king answers, "I am in great distress, for the Philistines are warring against me, and God has turned away from me and answers me no more" (28:15). Saul is of course correct, and Samuel speaks the word of the LORD to him as he had done while he lived. Saul has become the LORD's enemy, and God will now judge Saul and his sons (28:16–19).

The most interesting detail of the episode is the medium's word choice: she sees "a god" coming up out of the ground. The Hebrew word translated "god" is *elohim*, a term used more than 2,000 times for the true God, Yahweh of Israel. Why is the dead Samuel described with this word?

Despite being used for the God of Israel, the word *elohim* is not a label that uniquely refers to Yahweh. The term is used elsewhere of demons and divine members of Yahweh's unseen heavenly host (Deut 32:17; Ps 82:1). The word *elohim* is how biblical writers described a member of what we think of as the spiritual world. God is part of that world but is superior to all of its members (Exod 15:11; Isa 37:16, 20; Neh 9:6; Ps 136:2). Samuel's body had been entombed at Ramah (1 Sam 25:1; 28:3), but his spirit was living on the other side, in the realm of the dead—what we call the afterlife. All residents of that realm are described with the term *elohim* in the Old Testament.

This worldview was shared by Israel's neighbors.[1] The Hebrew phrase translated "medium" in 1 Samuel 28:7 is *ba'alath-ov* (literally, "mistress of the spirit of the dead"). The word *ov* refers to the human dead. This word occurs in Isaiah 19:3 in parallel to three other terms connected with the dead in the afterlife. One of these (*ittim*) is a close parallel to the Akkadian word for "ghost" (*etemmu*), a spirit of a deceased person that interacts with the living, human world.

The biblical writers believed in ghosts—the dead who lived on in the afterlife and could be contacted. But such contact was forbidden (Deut 18:9–14). The reason was not that it couldn't be done; it could. Rather, God insisted that he be the lone source of information from the spiritual world for his people. The command was for their own good—to prevent them from being deceived or harmed. The incident at Endor was exceptional, allowed by God for the purpose of reiterating his judgment of Saul.

> *The biblical writers believed in ghosts—the dead who lived on in the afterlife and could be contacted. But such contact was forbidden.*

25

The Politics of Marriage

When it comes to marriage, modern Western culture puts a premium on love. The notion is so ingrained that it's easy for us to presume that marriage worked the same way in biblical times. It often didn't. We need to resist romanticizing the relationships of biblical heroes and heroines—and that includes King David and his wives.

The Bible makes it clear that David was a polygamist (1 Sam 25:39–43; 2 Sam 5:13). This wasn't unusual for kings or those who desired kingship in ancient times. David took several wives, although this was not something God endorsed for kings (Deut 17:14–17). And a careful reading of the Old Testament tells us that David took multiple wives for political reasons.

David's first wife was Michal, the youngest daughter of King Saul (1 Sam 14:49). Saul gave Michal as a gift to David after David defeated Goliath (18:27–28). Although we are told Michal loved David, we are not told how David felt about her. But focusing too much on the sentiment might make us miss an important detail: The marriage put David in line for the kingship behind Saul's son Jonathan. When David became Saul's enemy, Saul took Michal away from David and gave her to another man (25:44). After

Saul's death, when David was on the verge of becoming king over all Israel, he demanded that Michal be returned to him before all the tribes could be joined under his rule (2 Sam 3:12–16).

David's wives Abigail and Ahinoam, his second and third wives respectively, are mentioned together in several passages (1 Sam 25:43–44; 2 Sam 2:2). First Samuel 14:50 identifies Ahinoam, daughter of Ahimaaz, as Saul's wife. It is possible that the Ahinoam who married Saul is the same Ahinoam that David took as a wife. David could have taken Saul's wife as his own in order to lay political claim to the rule of all 12 tribes. Even if David's Ahinoam was not Saul's wife, Nathan's denunciation of David years later, after David lusted for Bathsheba, indicates David had acquired other women who had been Saul's wives.

David's marriages were motivated by political strategy.

> I anointed you king over Israel, and I delivered you out of the hand of Saul. And I gave you your master's house and **your master's wives** into your arms and gave you the house of Israel and of Judah. (2 Sam 12:7–8)

When Abigail enters the biblical narrative (1 Sam 25), she is the wife of Nabal, whose name, appropriately, means "fool" in Hebrew. Nabal was very wealthy (1 Sam 25:1–2), the sort of wealth that would be expected of a territorial leader. He was also a Calebite (25:3), a descendant of Caleb. This seemingly innocuous detail sets the stage for David's eventual marriage to Abigail after Nabal's death.

In the time of Moses and Joshua, Caleb was given the city of Hebron and its nearby territory (Josh 14:12; 15:13-14). Hebron played an important role in David's life. It was one of the cities where he sought refuge as he fled from Saul (1 Sam 30:31), and it was the place where he was anointed king over Judah (2 Sam 2:11). First Chronicles 2:50-51 lists Bethlehem, the namesake of David's ancestral city, as a direct descendant of Caleb. David's coronation took place in Bethlehem, a city within the territory of the tribes of Benjamin and Judah, David's own tribe (2 Chr 11:5-12). After Saul's death, David began his own partial kingship over Judah and Benjamin, with Hebron as his capital. He reigned there for seven and a half years (2 Sam 5:5). David's anointing, reign, and coronation were, therefore, all associated with Calebite territory—and so was his wife Abigail, having been previously married to a prominent Calebite. By marrying Abigail, David joined the Calebite and Judahite lines in his rule from Hebron. The marriage made good political sense.

It's quite clear that David's marriages were motivated by political strategy—hardly something to emulate. But despite his epic failure to commit to one woman, as God intended, David was unfailingly loyal to Yahweh above all other gods. He never worshiped another. And for that, God chose David's line to be the conduit for the redemption of us all.

26

Defeating Ancient Foes

Goliath wasn't the only giant to fall in David's time. In 2 Samuel 21, David's mighty men defeat four Philistine warriors who are described as mammoth in size (21:16–22). Who were these giant men, and why is their defeat important? The answer lies in the backstory.

The unusually tall inhabitants of Canaan were called "Rephaim," alluding to warriors who were associated with supernatural evil prior to the great flood (Gen 6:4; Deut 2:10–11).[1] During the conquest, some of these giants, the Anakim—who were "counted as Rephaim" (Deut 2:11) due to their incredible stature—fled from Joshua's forces to the city of Gath (Josh 11:22; 13:3). These giants had still not been eradicated from the land by David's time; Goliath and the four giants David's men defeated were from Gath, the city of the Anakim (1 Sam 17:4; 2 Sam 21:22). Second Samuel 21:22 further specifies that the four giant men were descendants of giants (*ha-raphah*) from Gath.[2]

By taking out Goliath and four other giants, David and his men revisited the unfinished business of the conquest—the defeat of ancient foes.

This is not the only connection between the defeated giants and the Rephaim. The book of Joshua twice mentions "the valley of Rephaim," a valley that took its name from the presence of giant warriors (Josh 15:8; 18:16). The same valley is mentioned in 2 Samuel. In David's day, the valley got its name because the Philistines frequently used it as a base camp for their army (2 Sam 5:18, 22; 23:13). This valley was the location of several Israelite exploits and skirmishes with the Philistines (2 Sam 5:18; 23:13; 1 Chr 11:15). Among the Philistine ranks were giants from the city of Gath—Goliath and the four giant men, one of whom is described as Goliath's brother (1 Chr 20:5).

By taking out Goliath and four other giants, David and his men revisited the unfinished business of the conquest—the defeat of ancient foes. The biblical narrative therefore casts the establishment of David as king as counteracting this ancient evil.

27

Yahweh and His Asherah

Several inscriptions discovered in the 1970s refer to Yahweh in close association with "Asheratah" ('-sh-r-t-h).[1] This term is typically vocalized 'asheratah and is usually taken as a reference to the Canaanite goddess Asherah, mentioned in other ancient Semitic texts and the Old Testament. The relevant phrase in one inscription reads lyhwh shmrn wl 'shrth (literally, "to Yahweh of Samaria and to Asheratah").[2] In the Old Testament, the name of the goddess is spelled 'asherah. "Asheratah" and "Asherah" most likely refer to the same goddess. However, it is not actually clear whether these inscriptions intend to pair Yahweh with the goddess.[3]

Who Is Asherah?

Asherah was an important goddess in the mythology of the ancient city-state of Ugarit, located in what is now northern Syria. In the Ugaritic mythological texts, her name is spelled "Athiratu" (also spelled as "Athirat"); Asherah is the Hebrew spelling. Asherah and her husband El, the creator and high sovereign of the Ugaritic pantheon, were the parents of the gods of the pantheon. Athiratu/Asherah was thus the wife/consort of El.[4]

Asherah's connection to El is significant because 'el is one of the names of Israel's God. But 'el is a common, even standard, word for deity in Semitic languages, so its use in the Old Testament is not surprising. Nevertheless, the Old Testament writers do, for polemical reasons, appropriate motifs, imagery, and epithets from the Canaanite El to the God of Israel. The biblical writers wanted their readers to know that it was Yahweh who rightly deserved these lofty titles and exalted glory, not the Canaanite deity. Examples of borrowing between Israelite and Ugaritic religion include El's dwelling place (a well-watered garden [Eden] and sacred mountain [e.g., Eden in Ezek 28:13; Sinai, Zion]), the appending of "El" onto other divine names in the patriarchal era (e.g., El-Olam, El-Shaddai, El-Elyon), and titles like "Creator of heaven and earth" (Gen 14:19), and El as "divine warrior" (compare Exod 15:3). In other ways, the biblical writers are careful to distance Yahweh from the Canaanite El. The most well-known example is El's sexual prowess in the Ugaritic texts, none of which appears in the Old Testament with respect to the God of Israel.

Asherah/Athiratu should not be confused with another Semitic goddess Ashtart, also spelled Athtartu or Astarte.[5] The Ugaritic texts mention the goddess Ashtart nearly fifty times, while the mythological texts only rarely mention her, preferring Athiratu (that is, Asherah). Athtartu/Ashtart was one of Baal's consorts in Ugaritic mythology. The name Ashtart occurs fewer than ten times in the Old Testament (e.g., Judgs 2:13 as plural Ashtaroth; 1 Kgs 11:5, 33 as Ashtoreth), but the plural term Ashtaroth is often paired with the plural "Baals," which reflects the Ashtart-Baal coupling at Ugarit.

The Term *Asherah* in the Old Testament

The term *'asherah* appears roughly forty times in the Old Testament.[6] Most of these instances seem to refer to an object used in religious ceremonies, probably a tree or upright pole; one of the primary symbols for worship of the goddess Asherah was a sacred tree (e.g., Exod 34:13; Judges 3:7; 6:25–26; 1 Kgs 14:23; 2 Kgs 18:4). Sometimes the term clearly refers to the goddess Asherah herself (1 Kgs 18:19; 2 Kgs 23:4), but other passages blur or combine the two usages (e.g., compare 2 Kgs 21:3, 7).

"Yahweh and His Asherah"

The most famous inscriptions referring to "Yahweh and his *'asheratah*" come from a site located in the northern Sinai region known as Kuntillet Ajrud.[7] The texts date to ca. 800 BC or, in biblical history, the period of Israel's divided monarchy. In several of the inscriptions, the writer beseeches a blessing from "Yahweh ... and *'asheratah.*" The discovery (among others) prompted two questions: who or what is "Asheratah" in the inscription and what significance does the find have for understanding the religion of ancient Israel?

The term "Asheratah" in these inscriptions could be understood as a symbol associated with Yahweh—in which case, the lowercase should be used in the transliteration: "Yahweh and his *'asheratah.*" It could also be read as the name of the goddess Asherah, but it may refer to a symbol of the goddess Asherah—in which case, again, the lowercase spelling should be used.

If "*'asheratah*" is a symbol of Yahweh, then the phrase is a reference to Yahweh and some sort of object or shrine associated with him. Worshipers, perhaps, loosely associated a sacred tree with Yahweh; in the OT the God of Israel is associated with the tree of life in Eden (Yahweh's sacred space) and divine encounters with Yahweh are frequently marked by sacred trees (see Gen 12:6; 13:18; 18:1).[8] As a symbol for Yahweh, it could highlight his relationship to the divine being Wisdom in Prov 8:22–31, a passage that casts divine Wisdom as a co-creator.[9] In this case, there may be a connection with the husband-wife pairing of Athiratu and El from Ugarit. According to this view, Israelite monotheism over the course of its development gradually absorbed the goddess figure of Wisdom into Yahweh. The problem with this view is that no other ancient texts connect Asherah and the concept of divine Wisdom. Additionally, other gods (e.g., Marduk in Babylon) from the ancient Near East that absorb other deities in their ascendancy to supremacy specifically do not absorb goddesses.[10]

If the inscription points to the personal name Asherah, then whoever wrote the inscription believed that Yahweh had a wife.[11] The problem with this view is the final *h* (the Semitic letter *heh*) of the spelling would need to be read as a masculine suffix, rather than a feminine ending. The result would be "Yahweh and *his* asherah." However, rules of Hebrew word formation reject such a spelling for proper personal names. No personal name with such a suffix has ever been found in Hebrew, and it is extraordinarily rare in other west Semitic languages. The odds are

> *If the inscription points to the personal name Asherah, then whoever wrote the inscription believed that Yahweh had a wife.*

therefore very slim that the noun in the inscription is a personal name.

The idea that the inscription points to a symbol of the goddess Asherah, rather than to the goddess herself, could indicate that the writer believed that Yahweh had a consort wife or that Yahweh and Asherah were both deities and thus sought a blessing from both of them. This inscription could then be evidence of Israelite polytheism. The Old Testament frequently highlights (and condemns) Israelite worship of other gods and goddesses, particularly during the divided monarchy after the kingdom split following Solomon's death (the time when these inscriptions were written). An inscription from that period including the words "Yahweh and Asherah" would thus make sense. However, it is quite another thing to argue that this inscription proves "orthodox" Israelites once worshiped a goddess. The inscription offers no support for this idea.

28

Angels Aren't Perfect

Christians commonly think of angels as the good guys of the heavenly realm. The angels that sinned at the time of the flood and were cast into the underworld are, naturally, perceived as evil.[1] Consequently, many people separate the "fallen angels" from the "good" angels. They think of the latter as loyal, trustworthy servants of God, but that's only partly true.

Heavenly angelic beings are called "holy ones" in a number of places (Job 5:1; Ps 89:5, 7; Zech 14:5; Dan 4:13, 17; 8:13). Yet in Job, several passages allude to the possibility that God's angels aren't inherently perfect and holy:

> Even in his servants he puts no trust, and his angels he charges with error. (Job 4:18)

> Behold, God puts no trust in his holy ones, and the heavens are not pure in his sight. (Job 15:15)

> How then can man be in the right before God? How can he who is born of woman be pure? Behold, even the moon is not bright, and the stars are not pure in his eyes. (Job 25:4–5)

In Job 4:18, Eliphaz confidently reports that God accuses his own angels of error. There is no indication that the reference is to angels who are already in rebellion or estranged from God for transgressions in the distant past. Eliphaz is even more emphatic in Job 15. The heavens—or, to capture the parallelism more adequately, "heavenly ones"—simply aren't pure in his sight. If God doesn't even trust his heavenly entourage, how can Job expect God to accept him as pure and righteous (15:14–16)? Bildad's words in Job 25 echo Eliphaz's assessment exactly. In the Old Testament, references to the sun, moon, stars, or heavenly host sometimes allude to heavenly beings (Deut 4:19; 1 Kgs 22:19; 2 Kgs 21:3; Isa 14:13). Later in Job, these heavenly beings are said to have witnessed the creation of the world (Job 38:4–7) and are described using celestial language ("The morning stars sang together and all the sons of God shouted for joy").

> *If God doesn't even trust his heavenly entourage, how can Job expect God to accept him as pure and righteous?*

These unfavorable assessments of angels do not contradict the more positive portrayals of them elsewhere in Scripture. Angels are not "holy ones" due to moral perfection. In fact, this same term (*qadosh*; plural: *qedoshim*) is used in reference to people, who obviously lack inherent moral perfection (Pss 16:3; 34:9; Dan 8:24). Angels are called "holy ones" for a different reason: They serve in close proximity to God, the Holy One of Israel.

The truth is that the divine beings who share God's living space don't have a perfect track record. One such being was responsible for the first rebellion against God, opposing the Edenic plan of the Most High and seducing his human creations to sin (Gen 3; compare Rev 12:9; 20:2). This transgression was followed by the events of Genesis 6:1–4 (compare 2 Pet 2:4–5). A different group of heavenly "sons of God"—allowed to rule the nations as gods after the Tower of Babel judgment (Deut 32:8–9; compare 4:19–20)—later seduced the Israelites into idolatry and became corrupt (Ps 82; compare Deut 32:17).[2]

In simplest terms, God doesn't trust his holy ones because he knows better. But that doesn't completely capture the truth of these passages from Job. Angels aren't above moral and spiritual failure for a more fundamental reason: They don't possess God's nature or character—nor does any created intelligent being, human or divine. The possibility that any lesser being is allowed to occupy sacred space with the God of creation at all is a testimony to grace.

29

From Intercessors to Advocate

We seldom think of angels as intercessors, but the notion that they mediated between God and humans is an ancient one. The holy ones were part of God's assembled council (Ps 89:5-6; compare 82:1), which was conceived as a heavenly courtroom (Dan 7:10). Angels could even be called to testify before God and served to accuse, to plead on someone's behalf, or to pass judgment (Job 1:6-11; 11:7-10; 33:23-24).

Job's tragic circumstances evolve from contention in God's divine council—his heavenly host of the sons of God (Job 1:6-2:1)—instigated by the Adversary (*ha-satan*, often translated "Satan"), who challenges God's assessment of Job's unblemished character. In order to prove the Adversary wrong and vindicate his omniscience, God allows Job to suffer (1:9-12).

We know the rest of the story—at least the basic elements. Job's friends prove inept at comforting him; they even compound his suffering. Neither Job nor his friends know what has transpired behind the veil of heaven that led to Job's misery. The first friend, Eliphaz, tries to convince Job that he must have done something evil:

> Can mortal man be in the right before God? Can a man be pure before his Maker? Even in his servants he puts no trust, and his angels he charges with error. ... Call now; is there anyone who will answer you? To which of the holy ones will you turn? (Job 4:17–18; 5:1).

The jab is clear: Job, who are you to think you're righteous? Are you better than the angels? Will any of them intercede for you? Go ahead—make an appeal to one of the holy ones, the sons of God, who judge the affairs of men with and for God (Dan 7:9–10). Will any of them be on your side?

Scripture sometimes presents the angels' intercessory function in dramatic ways. In 1 Kings 22:19–23, we see the members of God's heavenly host debating how Ahab would best be led to his death after God had decreed it was time for the wicked king to go. One of the heavenly spirits comes up with a good strategy, and God approves it. In other places, decrees handed down by "the Most High" also are described as decrees of the watchers, the holy ones (Dan 4:13, 17, 24).

The ultimate significance of all this is found in the cross, which transforms the entire concept of advocacy before God. The question in Job 5:1 ("To which of the holy ones will you turn?") presumes that, if Job wants justice, he must get it from God, and that his case must be mediated by God's agents. The same thought is expressed later in the book: "If there

If Job wants justice, he must get it from God and his case must be mediated by God's agents—the angels.

be for [a man] an angel, a mediator, one of the thousand, to declare to man what is right for him ..." (33:23). This is the backdrop for Jesus' statement about "guardian" angels and children: "I tell you that in heaven their angels always see the face of my Father who is in heaven" (Matt 18:10).

Things are different now. Because of what Jesus did on the cross, we have direct access to God (Heb 4:16) through our new advocate, Jesus Christ (1 John 2:1)—the only mediator between God and humankind (1 Tim 2:5).

30

Jurassic Bible?

In the summer of 2015, I saw the movie *Jurassic World*, the latest installment of the Jurassic Park franchise based on the Michael Crichton novel by that name. The novel and the films center around the idea of bringing dinosaurs back from extinction by means of genetic engineering. It's a fascinating premise, especially since some paleontologists and geneticists are working on real-world procedures for accomplishing the feat. You can get a glimpse of the real science behind this work in the book *How to Build a Dinosaur* by Jack Horner, the paleontologist who partly inspired the film version of Dr. Alan Grant in *Jurassic Park*.[1]

One of the more interesting background elements in Horner's book is the story of Dr. Mary Schweitzer, who now teaches at North Carolina State University. When she began her journey into what would become her career, Schweitzer was a substitute teacher and mother of three. She gained Horner's permission to audit his vertebrate paleontology class at Montana State. The rest is history. Schweitzer got hooked and soon became Horner's protégé, earning a PhD in biology. She is now world-famous for discovering soft tissue in dinosaur bones that were 68 million years old. Young earth creationists thrilled to the discovery, touting it as incontrovertible proof that the earth is actually only thousands of years old, not millions since (they argue) soft tissue could never have survived that long.

There's just one problem with this picture. Schweitzer is an evangelical Christian—and she doesn't agree with the young earth creationists' use of her research. By her own testimony, she learned that a lot of what she'd heard in church about her field and about scientists wasn't true. But the experience didn't harm her faith; it made it stronger. Schweitzer is now an old earth creationist. This is no secret in the paleontological community. Her faith is as well-known as her discovery. Schweitzer is living proof that serious Christians can be serious scientists.

Mary Schweitzer is also living proof that honesty and integrity in letting the Bible be what it is and doing science matter. She isn't disputing the science behind the age of the bones she works on. She knows her field as well as anyone in the world. She isn't pretending that we need a young earth to believe in the authority of Scripture. She understands that the Bible is an ancient work inspired by God not to give us science, but to give us truth about things that can't be put under a microscope, like the spiritual world, our spiritual need, and our spiritual destiny if we believe God's plan for salvation. Those truths transcend science and aren't dependent on it. The Bible has a pre-scientific cosmology because God chose writers who lived in a pre-scientific age. He knew that would be no obstacle to communicating what he wanted communicated.

The Bible has a pre-scientific cosmology because God chose writers who lived in a pre-scientific age.

Schweitzer's testimony is useful for framing another example of how the Bible gets interpreted out of context to address a modern controversy: the teaching that there are dinosaurs in the Bible. The alleged evidence comes in the form of words like Leviathan (*lwytn*; Ps 104:26), Rahab (*rhb*; Isa 51:9), and Tannin, meaning "sea monster" or "dragon" (*tnyn*; Gen 1:21). This flawed notion isn't as disastrous as the "Bible teaching" that arose to account for newly discovered races from the 16th century onward that produced "biblical" racism. No one is going to be enslaved or die because people believe it. Its harm is less discernible. It gets filed with other ideas that are falsifiable and, once Christians learn that it isn't true, their faith in the Bible's inspiration will be damaged when it doesn't need to be.

How is this idea falsifiable? Context. As the *Lexham Bible Dictionary* article on "Leviathan" notes:

Leviathan is mentioned by name six times in the Hebrew Bible (Job 3:8; 41:1; Pss 74:14; 104:26; Isa 27:1). Most of these passages assert or allude to Yahweh's power and control over the sea monster. The mythological background of the deity battling and defeating a sea monster (i.e., the Chaoskampf ["chaos struggle"] motif) is most evident in Psa 74:14 and Isa 27:1. ... The mythological background of the Bible's references to Leviathan became apparent with the discovery of Ugaritic references to a sea monster called "Litan" (*ltn*).[2]

The Baal Cycle from Ugarit offers particularly precise parallels, as illustrated further in the same Bible dictionary article:

> The Baal Epic recounts how the storm god Baal displaced El as the chief deity of the Canaanite pantheon. The story involves Baal defeating Yam, the sea god. ... In this exchange, Mot refers to Baal's defeat of Litan (or Leviathan), apparently equating Yam and Litan (KTU 1.5, col. i, lines 1–8). ...
>
> > *When you killed Litan, the Fleeing Serpent,*
> > *Annihilated the Twisty Serpent,*
> > *The Potentate with Seven Heads,*
> > *The heavens grew hot, they withered.*
> > *But let me tear you to pieces,*
> > *Let me eat flanks, innards, forearms.*
> > *Surely you will descend into Divine Mot's throat,*
> > *Into the gullet of El's Beloved, the Hero.*
>
> The description of Litan in the first lines of this tablet from the Baal Epic use almost the exact words as the description of Leviathan in Isa 27:1.[3]

There are many additional parallels in ancient texts from Ugarit and elsewhere that illustrate the mythological connotations for those biblical terms.[4] The point I'm making here is that Leviathan and other "dinosaurs" are well-known mythological figures from uninspired texts outside the Bible contemporary with the biblical world. Pagan texts have their gods defeating these creatures to show their superiority or assert that their gods brought order over chaos at creation. But the Baal myth isn't literally true. Baal didn't really battle a dinosaur and become the god of all gods. These creatures are metaphors for the forces of chaos. Psalms 74:12–14 and 89:9–11 use this same metaphor to argue that it was Yahweh who subdued Leviathan / the sea dragon / Rahab to bring about creation order.[5] The point of these passages isn't that God was killing literal dinosaurs to transform the formless and empty world at creation. Rather, it was a polemic strategy to assert that Yahweh—not Baal or any other deity in the ancient world—was the Lord of creation and Most High God. Interpreting these terms in their original context means we don't have to fabricate "biblical meaning" to defend the Bible.

31

Proverbs: The Wisdom of Egypt?

Follow sound advice when you find it—that's the message the writer of Proverbs 22-23 wants his audience to ponder. He doesn't just tell his audience to "hear the words of the wise," though (22:17). He fulfills his own advice through literary means. In composing the passage, the writer draws on a piece of ancient Near Eastern literature: an Egyptian work known as the *Instruction of Amenemope*. This work, composed during the Ramesside period of the New Kingdom (ca. 1300-1000 BC), pre-dates the era of Solomon.

The *Instruction of Amenemope,* which was part of the ancient Egyptian wisdom genre of "instruction," was likely written by a scribe named Amenemope for instructing his own son. It was common for biblical writers to draw off the literary output of their neighbors in various ways. However, the writer of Proverbs doesn't just echo the words and wisdom of an Egyptian sage. He directs his readers to fear Yahweh, a feature of wise living that set Israelites apart from any other people group (Prov 1:7; 9:10).

Here is how Proverbs 22-23 compares with the ancient Egyptian work:

Proverbs	Content/ Theme	Amenemope[1]
Incline your ear, and hear the words of the wise, and apply your heart to my knowledge, for it will be pleasant if you keep them within you, if all of them are ready on your lips. (22:17–18)	*Appeal to be heard*	Give your ears, hear the sayings Give your heart to understand them; It profits to put them in your heart (III, 9–11)
Have I not written for you thirty sayings of counsel and knowledge (22:20)	*Follow these 30 wise sayings*	Look to these thirty chapters; They inform, they educate; They are the foremost of all books (XXVII, 7–8)
Do not rob the poor, because he is poor, or crush the afflicted at the gate (22:22)	*Don't rob the poor and afflicted*	Beware of robbing a wretch, Of attacking a cripple (IV, 4–5)
Make no friendship with a man given to anger, nor go with a wrathful man, (22:24)	*Don't make friends of hot-headed, violent people*	Do not befriend the heated man, Nor approach him for conversation. (XI, 13–14)

Proverbs	Content/ Theme	Amenemope
Do not move the ancient landmark that your fathers have set. (22:28) Do not move an ancient landmark or enter the fields of the fatherless, for their Redeemer is strong; he will plead their cause against you. (23:10–11)	*Don't move property markers*	Do not move the markers on the borders of fields, Nor shift the position of the measuring-cord. Nor encroach on the boundaries of a widow. (VII, 12–14)
When you sit down to eat with a ruler, observe carefully what is before you, and put a knife to your throat if you are given to appetite. Do not desire his delicacies, for they are deceptive food. (23:1–3)	*Dine with political rulers with caution*	Do not eat in the presence of an official And then set your mouth before him. If you are sated pretend to chew; content yourself with your saliva. Look at the bowl that is before you, And let it serve your needs. (XXIII, 13–18)

Proverbs	Content/Theme	Amenemope
Do not toil to acquire wealth; be discerning enough to desist. When your eyes light on it, it is gone, for suddenly it sprouts wings, flying like an eagle toward heaven. (23:4–5)	*Wealth is fleeting*	Do not strain to seek increase; What you have, let it suffice you. If riches come to you by theft, They will not stay the night with you. Comes day they are not in your house, Their place is seen but they're not there; Earth opened its mouth, leveled them, swallowed them. ... They made themselves wings like geese, and flew away to the sky. (IX, 14–X, 5)

Wisdom literature across the ancient Near East had a similar orientation toward instructing people on how to get along with others in society. Oftentimes, that advice arises from human experience and observation and proves relevant outside its original context because societies share similar experiences and settings for human interaction. For example, the advice about showing restraint and caution when dining with rulers applied to the Israelite as much as to the Egyptian (Prov 23:1–3; *Amenemope* XXIII, 13–18). We still find value in the book of Proverbs today for its solid ethical advice. The writer of Proverbs 22–23 recognized the words of wisdom found in the *Instruction of Amenemope* applied to his audience as well, though for the Israelite, instruction in wisdom was motivated by a healthy fear of Yahweh (Prov 15:33).

32

Heap Burning Coals on Their Heads

Our culture's preference for information in 140 characters or fewer is no modern invention. Ancient peoples shared our taste for brevity, as evidenced in the proverbs—short, pithy truisms about life. But brevity has its downsides. Sometimes we need more detail or context to understand a proverb's true message.

Proverbs 25:22 is a good example: "For you will heap burning coals on his head, and the Lord will reward you." Is this proverb Solomon's idea of "an eye for an eye"? I've heard more than one sermon that took that angle. Examining the wider context of this passage, however, shows that this is an unfortunate misinterpretation.

A Rebuttal to Retaliation

To better understand Proverbs 25:22, we need to read it in the context of the preceding verse:

> If your enemy is hungry, give him bread to eat, and if he is thirsty, give him water to drink, for you will heap burning coals on his head, and the LORD will reward you. (Prov 25:21–22)

Proverbs 25:21 gives no hint that revenge is an option for the wise person—one who fears the Lord (Prov 1:7; 9:10). Rather, this verse is a rebuttal to retaliation. Instead of suggesting that we seek vengeance, it encourages us to show kindness to our enemy: If he is hungry, feed him; if he is thirsty, give him water. This aligns with the wider biblical teachings on the treatment of enemies. For example, consider Proverbs 24:17–18:

> Do not rejoice when your enemy falls, and let not your heart be glad when he stumbles, lest the LORD see it and be displeased, and turn away his anger from him.

The Old Testament law likewise discourages us from seizing opportunities to harm our enemies: "If you meet your enemy's ox or his donkey going astray, you shall bring it back to him" (Exod 23:4). Both verses promote kindness toward enemies and hint that attitudes seeking harm for them are displeasing to God. This is a far cry from an eye-for-an-eye mentality.

Burning Shame

Another difficulty in understanding Proverbs 25:22 is the idea of heaping burning coals on someone's head. This is a foreign concept to modern readers. Cultural context can help here. Some interpreters see the burning coals as a metaphorical reference to an Egyptian custom whereby a person who had been shamed would bear a pan of smoldering coals on top of his head as an outward display of shame and regret.[1] Others see the language—which involves burning—as an expression of the inward burning of shame.

Proverbs uses the metaphor of burning fire elsewhere to describe the anguish of shame, as in the warnings about infidelity in Proverbs 6:27-28:

> Can a man carry fire next to his chest and his clothes not be burned?
>
> Or can one walk on hot coals and his feet not be scorched?

While we can't be completely sure which image or metaphor is in play, both capture the intent of Proverbs 25:22 well: By treating our enemies with kindness, we will put them to shame. Loving our enemies will make them ashamed of themselves and hopefully move them toward repentance (compare Matt 5:43-44). In this way, mercy is the best revenge.

33

Denial of the Afterlife

Ecclesiastes is a difficult book to read, let alone interpret. It's filled with statements that make you wonder what the writer was thinking. Take Ecclesiastes 9:5, for example:

> For the living know that they will die, but the dead know nothing, and they have no more reward, for the memory of them is forgotten.

This is just one of several passages in Ecclesiastes acknowledging the inevitability of death.[1] But this verse is particularly troublesome. Does it teach that there is no conscious afterlife? Exploring other Old Testament passages about the afterlife can help us understand what the biblical writer was really saying here.

Looking Outside of Sheol

Studies of the Old Testament notion of an afterlife are often restricted to passages using the word *sheol* (the Hebrew word for the realm of the dead).[2] This has led to the erroneous conclusion that the OT lacks the notion of a *positive*, conscious afterlife for believers. But if we expand our focus, we'll find that it does contain hints of a conscious afterlife.

For instance, when contemplating death, the psalmist says, "Nevertheless, I am continually with you; you hold my right hand. ... [A]fterward you will receive me to glory. ... God is the strength of my heart and my portion forever" (Ps 73:23–24, 26). The idea of "upholding," which is present in the phrase "holding of the hand," is elsewhere associated with God's presence: "But you have upheld me because of my integrity, and set me in your presence forever" (Ps 41:12). Although we could conclude that the psalmist here is claiming that he'll live an everlasting life on earth or that the language here is an exaggeration, it's better to view this passage as expressing hope of everlasting life in the presence of God—a life that transcends this one.

The law's prohibition against contacting the disembodied (human) dead (Deut 18:11) also provides support for the Old Testament idea of a conscious afterlife. In ancient times it was thought that the dead, as members of the spiritual world, could provide information that was otherwise unobtainable. The Bible prohibits contacting the dead not because doing so was impossible, but because it *was* possible (1 Sam 28:13); God doesn't command people to avoid doing things that are impossible. Rather than seeking insight from the dead, the godly were to seek divine knowledge directly from God or through means that God had provided, such as the Urim and Thummim, the ephod, and the prophets.

Fallen Asleep

The frequent descriptions of dying as being "gathered" to one's "people" or as having "slept" with one's "fathers" provides further insight into the Old Testament notion of the afterlife.³ From his deathbed, Jacob told his sons, "I am to be gathered to my people; bury me with my fathers in the cave that is in the field of Ephron the Hittite" (Gen 49:29). First Kings 2:10 similarly reads, "Then David slept with his fathers and was buried in the city of David." At first glance, the description of the dead as "sleeping" appears to suggest an unconscious afterlife. But archaeology demonstrates that references to sleeping actually refer to the posture of the body in burial—not a denial of a conscious afterlife. Archaeological studies of burial practices have also shown that people in the biblical period buried their dead with objects for use in the afterlife.⁴ This, along with the biblical characters' requests to be buried with the remains of their family members, strongly suggests that ancient Israelites believed they would share an afterlife with their dead family members.

Detached, Not Unconscious

So if Ecclesiastes 9:5 isn't speaking of the lack of a conscious afterlife, what is it talking about? A parallel passage in 2 Kings 22:20 can help answer that. In this passage, God tells Josiah through the prophetess Huldah: "Therefore, behold, I will gather you to your fathers, and you shall be gathered to your grave in peace, and your eyes shall not see all the disaster that I will bring upon this place." Like Ecclesiastes 9:5, this passage speaks of the dead lacking knowledge. But this verse doesn't say that Josiah, upon death, would know nothing at all—it simply means that he wouldn't know what was happening on earth. Similarly, Ecclesiastes 9:5 likely refers to the dead being detached from conscious participation in this world, not an unconscious afterlife.

34

Solomon's Bride or Jesus' Bride?

The Song of Solomon is one of the most controversial books in the Bible. Most people reading it for the first time wonder how it ever got in the Bible—and why. At least a half dozen explanations for Song of Solomon's inclusion in the canon have been proposed since ancient times.[1] In today's Christian context, Bible students usually opt for one of two options (or both).

Many modern believers consider Song of Solomon to be a celebration of marital intimacy. But this interpretation is easier said than demonstrated. Anyone who has closely read Song of Solomon knows it's nearly impossible to discern a clear storyline. In addition, a good case can be made that, if you try to read the book chronologically, the lovers engage in sexual intimacy (Song 1:4, 13, 17; 2:4–6; 3:4) prior to the wedding night (Song 4:1–5:1). Most scholars today see the book as an anthology of love poetry, noting its similarity to ancient poetry of this type—especially Egyptian love poetry.[2] So if you're not married to (pardon the pun) seeing the book as a linear story, you can still embrace it as a celebration of the act of marriage.

In ancient times, the view that the book was about erotic relations (even within marriage) wasn't the default perspective. In the Judaism of the first few centuries of the Christian era (AD), the view that the book was an allegory about God's love for Israel/Jerusalem rose to prominence. That approach ultimately influenced early Christian interpreters to regard the book as an allegory for Christ's love for his bride, the Church.[3] However, in my judgment, this second approach is the least likely to be correct. My skepticism is driven by a simple litmus test: Does a New Testament writer ever quote Song of Solomon to make this point? No. In fact, the Song of Solomon is never quoted in the New Testament.

If Song of Solomon is an allegory for Christ's love for the Church, the New Testament writers had many opportunities to draw from it. The language of bride and bridegroom appears nearly two dozen times in the New Testament, several of which appear to reference the Church (e.g., Rev 19:7; 21:9). Jesus is referred to as the "bridegroom" (John 3:29; Mark 2:19); the "marriage supper of the Lamb" (Rev 19:6–10) is a clear allusion to the time when believers are finally in Jesus' presence. In Ephesians 5:22–25 Paul specifically uses the relationship of Christ and the Church to talk about marriage:

> Wives, submit to your own husbands, as to the Lord. For the husband is the head of the wife even as Christ is the head of the church, his body, and is himself its Savior. Now as the church submits to Christ, so also wives should submit in everything to their husbands. Husbands, love your wives, as Christ loved the church and gave himself up for her.

Yet nowhere in this passage—or anywhere else in the NT—do we find imagery from Song of Solomon. The New Testament writers' decision not to use Song of Solomon demonstrates there is no basis for presuming Song of Solomon is about Christ's love for his Church. The later Bible interpreters who promoted this view weren't more in tune with the Spirit than those guided to write the New Testament under inspiration.

Ultimately, we must remember that, like every other book of the Bible, Song of Solomon was written for us, but not to us. Its meaning isn't something that only became clear once Christ had come and the Church had been born. Its context wasn't something far in the future. Rather, the book's poetic celebration of marital intimacy highlights God's good gift to those who bear his image.

If Song of Solomon is an allegory for Christ's love for the Church, why didn't the New Testament writers ever make that connection?

35

Gog of the Supernatural North

The enigmatic Gog, the terrible invader of Israel (Ezek 38:2–3, 6, 15; 39:1–2) is one of the more mysterious figures in the Bible. There is no consensus about the identity of Gog. Even ancient sources found him as much a conundrum as we do today.

Let the Guessing Begin

There hasn't been any shortage of conjectures about Gog's identity. The leading guesses are Gagi, a little-known prince mentioned in Assyrian annals as ruling people in the mountains north of Assyria, and Gyges, the ancient king of Lydia. Both have been rejected by most scholars, mainly because what is known of these figures fails to conform with the details we find in Ezekiel.[1]

Lack of a secure historical reference point for Gog has led to speculative identifications from modern history. One of the most widely circulated is that Gog should be associated with Russia—a view that draws on several arguments. Gog is identified in Ezekiel 38:2 as "the chief prince of Meshech and Tubal" (*nesi rosh meshekh wethuval*) who comes from "the uttermost parts of the north" (Ezek 38:15). Meshech and Tubal, it is argued, sound similar to Moscow and Tobolsk, and Russia is certainly far north in relation to the land of Israel. The Hebrew term translated "chief prince," *nesi rosh*, was rendered *archonta Rōs* ("commander of Ros") in the Septuagint, the Greek translation of the Old Testament. This translation understands the Hebrew term *rosh* to be the name of the place Gog ruled, and "Ros" sounds like another place name—Russia.

But identifying Gog as Russia is exegetically indefensible. Just because two words sound similar in two different languages doesn't mean those words have the same meaning. In transliteration, Hebrew *yam* looks and sounds the same as the English word "yam," but the former refers to a body of water while the latter describes an edible plant. Hebrew *rosh*, Greek *Rōs*, and English "Russia" have

> *Identifying Gog as Russia is exegetically indefensible.*

no relationship to each other. Further, Genesis 10:2 locates Meshech and Tubal in Anatolia (modern Turkey), not Russia (compare Ezek 27:12–15).

The main problem with the Russia theory, though, is the fact that *nesi rosh* should not be understood as "commander of Ros," but as either "chief prince" or "the prince, the chief." The full phrase identifying Gog (*nesi rosh meshekh wethuval*) means either the "chief prince of Meshech and Tubal" or "the prince (that is, the chief) of Meshech and Tubal."

A Better Strategy

Gog is described as an invader from the north (*tsaphon*). This is an important detail; after all, when Assyria and Babylon destroyed the kingdoms of Israel and Judah, they both invaded from the north. As a result, Israelites feared northern invaders. They also feared the north because it was considered the domain of Baal, whose home was Mount Zaphon (called *tsaphanu* in Canaanite, the equivalent of Hebrew *tsaphon* or "north").

It is no wonder, then, that the "king of the north" emerges in the book of Daniel as the antichrist figure (the "little horn"; Dan 7–8). Most scholars agree on the king's identity at this point, since the exploits of the king of the north in Daniel 11 closely mirror those of the awful tyrant Antiochus IV, a Greek ruler whose kingdom was in Syria and who considered himself an exalted deity. In the second century BC, Antiochus forced Jewish priests to sacrifice unclean animals on the temple altar. Daniel 11:36–37 describe Antiochus well: "He shall exalt himself and magnify himself above every god, and shall speak astonishing things against the God of gods."

Because of the king of the north, many scholars believe Gog might be another way of describing either Antiochus or the future antichrist who was prefigured by Antiochus. This fits well with the Baal association, since "prince Baal" (*baal zebul* in Canaanite) served as a title for Satan (*beelzebul*; Matt 10:25). These links have led some scholars to believe that Gog comes from the ancient Sumerian word *gûg* ("darkness"). It may well be that Ezekiel wasn't thinking about a historical person when he prophesied about Gog. Instead, he might have envisioned a satanic figure from the dark, supernatural north.

36

Filtering God

The Old Testament tells us that no person can see the face of God and live (Exod 33:20). The New Testament echoes this prohibition (John 1:18). The prophet Hosea, however, seems to disagree. In Hosea 12:3–4, the prophet revisits the story of Jacob as told in Genesis:

> In the womb he [Jacob] deceived his brother,
>> and in his manhood he struggled with God.
> He struggled with the angel and prevailed;
>> he pleaded for his mercy.
> He met him at Bethel,
>> and there he spoke with him. (LEB)

If we turn back to Genesis, we find that Jacob "struggled" (*sarah*) with "a man" in a physical scuffle (Gen 32:24 LEB). The same Hebrew word is also used in Hosea 12:3 for Jacob's struggle with God, thereby linking these two passages. As Jacob wrestled the stranger, he came to realize he was struggling with God (*elohim*) in human form (Gen 32:28). He named the place "Peniel" (meaning, "the face of God" in Hebrew), expressing amazement that he had been allowed to live (32:30). This incident led Jacob to rededicate himself to God at Bethel (35:1–7), where he had first seen God in a vision (28:10–22).

Hosea 12:3–4 summarizes this series of events in Jacob's life and confirms the divine identity of his opponent by saying Jacob "struggled with God." But Hosea takes it one step further: Jacob "struggled with God" *and* with an angel (*mal'ak*) during that combat. Yet again, the word "struggled" is another form of the same Hebrew word (*sor*).[1] Here, Hosea is asserting that a certain angel in the Old Testament was the God of Israel in human form.

> *A certain angel in the Old Testament was the God of Israel in human form.*

Later in Genesis, when Jacob was at the end of his life, he blessed the sons of Joseph. In the blessing, Jacob uses the terms for God and angel in parallel as though they are the same being. In Hebrew, the verb translated "may he bless" is grammatically *singular*, confirming the writer saw the two terms as referring to *the same being*.

> The God (*elohim*) before whom my fathers, Abraham and Isaac, walked,
>> The God (*elohim*) who shepherded me all my life unto this day,
>> The angel (*mal'ak*) who redeemed me from all evil,
>> *may he bless* the boys. (Gen 48:15–16 LEB)

So, is there a contradiction between the verses in Genesis and Hosea and those in Exodus and the Gospel of John that say people are forbidden from seeing the face of God? The key is in the translation of the Hebrew word used for "face" in these passages. The Hebrew word translated "face" in Exodus 33:20 is *panim*, which colloquially means God's *presence*. Old Testament passages that make this declaration actually state that no one can see the *presence* of God unveiled. That privilege was reserved for those in heaven— such as Jesus before coming to earth (John 1:18).

God's presence had to be filtered for humanity. In the Old Testament, God sometimes chose the filter of human form (the angel) so he could speak with people. They saw the face of the angel but were protected from direct contact with the presence of God. In the fullness of time, this was accomplished even more dramatically through the incarnation of Jesus—Immanuel, "God with us" (Matt 1:23).

37

God of Fire and Storm

God is the central character in many Bible passages. This should come as no surprise to us. How his presence is depicted, however, can be quite unexpected. We typically think of God as an invisible spirit, as Jesus describes him in John 4:24, or as a man, even before Jesus was born (e.g., Gen 18; 28:10-22; Exod 23:20-23). But Habakkuk pictures him differently:

> God came from Teman, and the Holy One from Mount Paran. His splendor covered the heavens, and the earth was full of his praise. His brightness was like the light; rays flashed from his hand; and there he veiled his power. ... You stripped the sheath from your bow, calling for many arrows. You split the earth with rivers. The mountains saw you and writhed; the raging waters swept on; the deep gave forth its voice; it lifted its hands on high. The sun and moon stood still in their place at the light of your arrows as they sped, at the flash of your glittering spear. (Hab 3:3-4, 9-11)

The portrait of God as Divine Warrior in Habakkuk 3 is a theophany—an appearance of God. Old Testament theophanies can be frightening. This particular one harks back to Mount Sinai, where the Israelites witnessed the appalling power and overwhelming glory of God who arrived with "thunders and lightnings and a thick cloud" to speak to Moses and the people (Exod 19:16). The mountain trembled and was "wrapped in smoke" when God descended on it "in fire" (19:18).

Prophets like Habakkuk who call up the "flashing fiery mountain" imagery wanted their readers to experience the emotion and fear of the Sinai encounter, an event that precipitated the conquering of the promised land. But this military metaphor is not all Habakkuk has in mind. A close look at the weaponry symbolism turns the focus.

The most common type of Old Testament theophany relies on the phenomena of nature—lightning, thunder, dark clouds, flooding, hailstones, and violent winds. To the people of the ancient biblical world, these natural forces were a terrifying mystery. They were also an essential part of survival, since the storms brought life-giving rain and subsequent good crops. Habakkuk 3 contains several "storm theophany" elements used throughout the Old Testament: God riding on a chariot through the heavens and through thick, dark clouds (Pss 18:11; 104:3)—commanding the winds and sending thunder and "arrows" of lightning, which he wields like weapons (Job 36:29–30; Ps 77:17–18; Zech 9:14). Second Samuel 22 combines all these elements in a similar way:

He made darkness around him his canopy, thick clouds, a gathering of water. Out of the brightness before him coals of fire flamed forth. The LORD thundered from heaven, and the Most High uttered his voice. And he sent out arrows and scattered them; lightning, and routed them. Then the channels of the sea were seen; the foundations of the world were laid bare at the rebuke of the LORD, at the blast of the breath of his nostrils. (2 Sam 22:12–16)

Prophets like Habakkuk wanted to connect their audience to the Sinai encounter; they also wanted to communicate that God is the creator and master of the natural forces that both terrified and sustained them. He can summon the elements—rain, hail or fire—and make the earth tremble and split. The message is simple but profound. God is not only the awesome power behind nature—He is greater than those incomprehensible forces. He can control that power and use it to punish or provide. He can wipe out the enemies of His people with the maelstrom, or throttle that fury to preserve life. When He speaks, we should listen.

> *God is not only the awesome power behind nature—He is greater than those incomprehensible forces.*

38

Zechariah's Divine Messiah

Jerusalem is under siege. The city is caught in a raging battle against "all the nations of the earth" (Zech 12:3). This battle, part of an oracle in the book of Zechariah, is reminiscent of the book of Revelation (Zech 12; compare Rev 16:14; 20:9). Yet, instead of being a dismal scene, the story is one of hope for the people of God, as Yahweh himself declares that he will "seek to destroy all the nations that come against Jerusalem" (Zech 12:9). Amid this Armageddon-like destruction is an allusion to a future, pierced messiah (Zech 12:10; compare John 19:37). This is no ordinary savior.

> And the LORD will give salvation to the tents of Judah first, that the glory of the house of David and the glory of the inhabitants of Jerusalem may not surpass that of Judah. On that day the LORD will protect the inhabitants of Jerusalem, so that the feeblest among them on that day shall be like David, **and the house of David shall be like God, like the angel of the LORD, going before them.** And on that day I will seek to destroy all the nations that come against Jerusalem. (Zech 12:7–9)

Zechariah 12:8 declares that the "house of David"—referring to a future king from the royal dynastic line of David—will be "like God, like the angel of the LORD." To grasp the significance of this verse, we need to recognize the parallelism between God and the angel of the LORD.[1] Jewish readers would have known that God and the angel of the LORD are identified with each other in passages throughout the OT. Earlier, I noted how Hosea identified the angel of the LORD with God himself (*elohim*) on the basis of Genesis.[2] Zechariah 12:8 also casts David's heir as like God (*elohim*) and as like the angel of the LORD.

Wanting to identify David's heir with God and the angel who is God in human form, Zechariah describes this future heir as "going before" God's people into battle and "destroying all the nations" that threaten Jerusalem (Zech 12:9–10). This is precisely the role of the angel of the LORD—the angel in whom the essence of Yahweh himself dwells (see Exod 23:20–23).[3] In Judges 2:1–2, after the death of Joshua, it is the angel of the LORD who, using first person language, appears and claims to have driven out the enemy inhabitants of the promised land (Judg 2:1–2). Elsewhere God's own presence receives this credit (Deut 4:37). God and the angel of the LORD are one—divinely fighting for God's people.

The Old Testament prophet not only foresaw a crucified Davidic king, but an heir of David who was God in human form.

This angel is God in human form—and the heir of David in Zechariah is identified the same way. The Old Testament prophet not only foresaw a crucified Davidic king, but an heir of David who was God in human form. Remarkably, this identification also shows up in the New Testament, in precisely the same context. Jude 5 tells us that it was "Jesus, who saved a people out of the land of Egypt, [and] afterward destroyed those who did not believe." Jesus, the pierced messiah, is associated with the angel of the LORD. And he is no ordinary savior.[4]

Part Three

New Testament

39

Mark's Use of Isaiah

Mark's opening words are the brilliant launch of a masterful presentation of the arrival and ministry of Jesus. As the re-manifestation of God in the form of a mortal man, he will lead Israel out of bondage and establish an earthly kingdom that will, as the prophets foretold, include all nations of the earth. Mark's presentation isn't new, though. Starting with this first citation, Mark models his presentation of Jesus after statements found in Isaiah.

Mark: Introduction to His Account of Jesus	
Mark Announces King and Kingdom	*Isaiah Speaks to Captive Israel*
Mark 1:3-4 (introducing John the Baptist) ³ the **voice of one crying in the wilderness: 'Prepare the way of the Lord, make his paths straight,'** ⁴ John appeared, baptizing in the wilderness ...	**Isaiah 40:3 (introducing the herald of Yahweh's return)** ³ A voice cries: **"In the wilderness prepare the way of the LORD; make straight in the desert a highway** for our God."

Mark 1:9–11 (baptism of Jesus)	Isaiah 9:1; 64:1; and 42:1 (the Spirit-anointed Servant arrives)
[9] In those days Jesus came from Nazareth of **Galilee** and was baptized by John **in the Jordan**. [10] And when he came up **out of the water**, immediately he saw **the heavens being torn open** and **the Spirit descend[ed]** on him ...	[9:1] ... in the latter time [God] has made glorious the way of the sea, the land beyond **the Jordan**, **Galilee** of the nations ... [64:1] Oh that you [**God**] would **rend the heavens** and **come down**, that the mountains might quake at your presence ... [42:1] Behold, my servant ... I have put **my Spirit** upon him ...
Mark 1:12–13 (Jesus suffers in the wilderness)	Isaiah 32:14–16 (Israel is desolate, awaiting rebirth)
[12] The Spirit immediately drove him out into **the wilderness**. [13] And he was in **the wilderness** forty days, being tempted by Satan. And he was with the wild animals ...	[14] For the palace is forsaken, the populous city deserted; the hill and the watchtower will become dens forever ... a pasture of flocks [15] until the Spirit is poured upon us from on high, and **the wilderness** becomes a fruitful field ... [16] Then justice will dwell in **the wilderness** ...
Mark 1:14–15 (Jesus preaches the good news of God's kingdom)	Isaiah 52:7; 61:1 (the good news of God's reign)
[14] ... **Jesus** came into Galilee, **proclaiming the gospel of God**, [15] and saying, "The time is fulfilled, and the **kingdom of God** is at hand; **repent and believe in the gospel**."	[52:7] How beautiful upon the mountains are the feet of **him who brings good news**, who publishes peace, **who brings good news** of happiness, who **publishes salvation**, who says to Zion, "**Your God reigns**." [61:1] ... the LORD has anointed me **to bring good news** ...

Mark's use of Isaiah to introduce Jesus as the returning Yahweh is hard to miss—if we know what we're looking at. And he continues tracking with Isaiah through the rest of his account.

Mark: The Purpose and Fact of Jesus' Suffering and Death	
Mark 10:45 (purpose) ⁴⁵"For even the Son of Man came not to be served but **to serve**, and **to give his life as a ransom** for many."	**Isaiah 53:11 (purpose of the Servant's suffering)** ¹¹... by his knowledge shall the righteous one, **my servant, make many to be accounted righteous, and he shall bear their iniquities.**
Mark 10:33–34 (suffering and death) ³⁴ "And they will **mock** him and **spit** on him, and **flog** him and **kill** him. And after three days he will rise."	**Isaiah 50:6; 53:12 (Servant's suffering and death)** ⁵⁰:⁶ **I gave my back to those who strike** ... I hid not my face from **disgrace** and **spitting**. ⁵³:¹² ... **he poured out his soul to death** ...
Mark 11:17; 13:10 (extent of the gospel) ¹¹:¹⁷ And he was teaching them and saying to them, "Is it not written, '**My house shall be called a house of prayer for all the nations**'? But you have made it a den of robbers." ¹³:¹⁰ "And **the gospel must first be proclaimed to all nations**."	**Isaiah 56:6–7 (vision of the future kingdom)** ⁶ And the foreigners who join themselves to the LORD ... to love the name of the LORD ... ⁷ these I will bring to my holy mountain, and make them joyful in **my house** of prayer; their burnt offerings and their sacrifices will be accepted on my altar; for **my house shall be called a house of prayer for all peoples.**"

Mark's use of Isaiah is stunning, but not unique. Each gospel writer created a deliberate, strategic work with its own agenda to present Jesus as the fulfillment of God's Old Testament promises. For Mark, Isaiah's prophecies were the perfect vehicle for presenting the good news of Jesus.

40

Demons, Swine, and Cosmic Geography

> He lived among the tombs. And no one could bind him anymore, not even with a chain, for he had often been bound with shackles and chains, but he wrenched the chains apart, and he broke the shackles in pieces. No one had the strength to subdue him. Night and day among the tombs and on the mountains he was always crying out and cutting himself with stones. (Mark 5:3–5)

This vivid description begins one of the most dramatic stories in the Gospels—the account of Jesus' exorcism of the man possessed by Legion. The story and its imagery are so unique that scholars have debated Mark's motive for including it in his Gospel. One theory is that Mark wanted to give hope to people suffering from mental illness. While the story does describe the man as being restored to "his right mind" after the exorcism (5:15), this modern reading is undermined by the clarity of the account itself. The man was possessed by demons with whom Jesus conversed (5:6–10). The text explicitly says that demons caused the swine to run to their deaths in the sea (5:11–13). This emphasis on demons leaves little room for another interpretation.

Other scholars believe that the story is a cryptic call for political liberation. The support for this interpretation is wrapped up in the terms Mark uses: The name Legion (*legiōn*) is a direct reference to Roman forces, and the term used for the swine (*agelē*, "herd") is also used of Roman recruits. However, at this time Jews wouldn't have been earnestly seeking Roman expulsion from Gentile areas, so it's difficult to see this being Mark's intention.

Ultimately, these interpretations miss the cosmic-symbolic messaging of the incident. Immediately before this exorcism, Jesus rebuked the wind and waves as he crossed the Sea of Galilee (4:35–40)—an act that cast him as the God of the Old Testament who had power over the sinister forces of cosmic chaos (Ps 89:8–9).[1] Prior to Mark 5, Jesus had restricted his preaching and miraculous displays of power to a Jewish audience. He was, after all, Israel's Messiah. His focus changes in 5:1 when he deliberately enters the country of the Gerasenes—Gentile territory. The mention of swine further associates this region with Gentiles (Lev 11:7).

Mark's report of Legion's question—"What have you to do with me?" (Mark 5:7)—creates a connection between Jesus' entrance into Gentile land and his earlier ministry to the Jews. Legion's question echoes the cries of the unclean spirits Jesus cast out in Mark 1:24 when he was in the Jewish region of Galilee. But there is a subtle difference between the demons' exclamations—one that identifies Mark's theological point in the Legion account: In Mark 1:24, the unclean spirits address their foe as "Jesus of Nazareth." But in 5:7, Legion identifies Jesus as "Son of the Most High." The title "Most High" reflects the Old Testament theology of cosmic geography. Recall that in Deuteronomy 32:8–9, the "Most High" had disinherited the nations of the world, assigned them to the dominion of supernatural sons of God, and then created Israel as his own inheritance.[2] Those sons of God rebelled and became corrupt (Ps 82:1–4), throwing God's order into chaos (Ps 82:5).

The Messiah, the Son of God, is not only here to redeem Israel. He is here to begin repossessing the Gentile nations as his own

What we have in Mark 5 is more than an exorcism and suicidal swine. We have a strong theological message. The Messiah, the Son of God, is not only here to redeem Israel. He is here to begin repossessing the Gentile nations as his own. Reclaiming the nations will require the defeat of the powers of darkness. Jesus' exorcism of Legion begins that campaign—something he'll complete when he returns (Ps 82:6–8; Isa 34:1–4).

41

Strange and Powerful Signs

The Gospels variously record several unusual events that occurred in conjunction with the death and resurrection of Jesus: the tearing of the temple veil, an earthquake, the opening of local tombs and the resurrection of their occupants, and darkness covering the land (Matt 27:51–56; Mark 15:38–41; Luke 23:44–49). Why did the writers include these details? Although interpreters have suggested theories for each occurrence, these events are best understood as a whole, collectively presenting a picture of God's judgment of a world thrown into chaos at the fall, as well as affirming the promise of Edenic restoration.

Most commentators consider the tearing of the veil and its related darkness and earthquake to signify that the old system of law and sacrifice had become obsolete with the death and subsequent resurrection of the Messiah. While this understanding would become evident later in the history of the early church, it is not at all clear that people in the first century would have interpreted these strange occurrences in this way. It is more likely that those who experienced what the gospel writers describe would have thought of the cosmic forces of chaos—the disorder that is implied before God's act of creation in Genesis 1 and that overwhelmed the world after rebellion in Eden.

The formless and empty earth is characterized by darkness (Gen 1:2), as is the realm of the dead (Job 10:21; 17:11–16; 38:17; Ecc 11:8). The shaking of the foundations of the earth is a familiar description of the world not being the way it was intended at creation (Ps 104:5), and the shaking indicates God's judgment on that disorder (Pss 18:7, 15; 82:5). The first-century Jewish historian Josephus noted that, for many Jews, the design and partitioning of the tabernacle tent (and so the temple) was the pattern of the ordered universe.[1] Consequently, when darkness, earthquake, and the tearing of the veil accompanied the death of Jesus, Jews of his day would have feared the end of the world—the victory of chaos. The signs three days later would have alerted them that a new age was at hand.

> *When darkness, earthquake, and the tearing of the veil accompanied the death of Jesus, Jews of his day would have feared the end of the world.*

Matthew's strange account of tombs opening and raised bodies of the "saints" (literally, "holy ones") coming forth would have drawn people's attention to Old Testament passages that foretold of resurrection at the day of the Lord—the time when God would set all things right (Dan 12:2–3; Isa 26:19; Ezek 37:1–10).[2] The result of God's judgment "on the great day of God the Almighty" (Rev 16:14 ESV) would be a reset for the whole world—a return to the unspoiled perfection of Eden, this time on a global scale (Rev 21–22). The new earth will have no darkness (Rev 21:25; 22:5), and death will be banished (Rev 21:4)—ideas familiar to Jews of Jesus' day (Hos 13:14; Isa 60:19-20).

Of course, Jesus' resurrection is the ultimate sign of the world's redemption and the linchpin of the Christian faith. Because Christ was raised, we have assurance that we will be raised (1 Cor 15:20-22). However, the significance of Jesus' resurrection is not limited to being the solution for human mortality. As the second or "last" Adam, Jesus reverses the first Adam's failure in Eden (1 Cor 15:45-48). Jesus' resurrection is frequently linked with the overthrow of the principalities and powers that govern the nations disinherited by God since Babel (Deut 32:8-9; Col 2:13-15; 1 Cor 14:20-28; Eph 1:15-23), bringing the Gentiles back into God's family through the gospel. The events that accompany Jesus' death—darkness, the earthquake, the torn veil, the opened tombs—set the stage for the restorative power of his resurrection, signaling the return of Eden on a global scale.

42

Is Exorcism for Everyone?

A recent survey of one thousand American adults found that more than half believe that demons can possess people.[1] The New Testament of course contains clear testimony of demon-possession and Jesus' power to exorcise demons. Mark's Gospel has one of the most dramatic accounts—the confrontation between Jesus and Legion (Mark 5:1–20).[2] While this episode in the ministry of Jesus is well known, something else the Lord says about demons is equally remarkable but gets much less attention:

> And these signs will accompany those who believe: in my name they will cast out demons; they will speak in new tongues; they will pick up serpents with their hands; and if they drink any deadly poison, it will not hurt them; they will lay their hands on the sick, and they will recover. (Mark 16:17–18)

I know I'm a believer; I'm trusting in Jesus' work on the cross on my behalf for my eternal destiny. But I've never cast out a demon, and I don't want to test whether I'm immune to poison or venomous snakes. Is this passage really saying that every Christian should be exorcizing demons, handling serpents, and ingesting lethal toxins? Some Christians think so, but Scripture itself indicates that this is a misreading of the passage.

Many scholars view Mark 16 as foreshadowing miraculous acts that the apostles would perform after Jesus' resurrection—signs that validated their message about Jesus. In Acts 28:3–6, Paul was bitten by a viper, but the poisonous venom had no effect on him. The book of Acts also reports in very broad terms that the apostles performed miraculous signs and wonders (14:3; 19:11, 12, 17; 28:8), including exorcism of demons (5:12–13). It's not unreasonable to presume that resistance to poisons also might have been part of this picture (although it is not mentioned specifically). In fact, ancient Jewish texts allude to worshipers of God being protected from poisoned food.[3]

Is this passage really saying that every Christian should be exorcizing demons, handling serpents, and ingesting lethal toxins?

The events of Acts are important for understanding Mark 16:17–18. When these gifts of power are mentioned, they are connected to the apostles. We know as well that the impartation of the Holy Spirit—the source of spiritual gifts—came by the apostles laying hands on believers (Acts 8:17–19; Rom 1:11). One such instance involved the gift of tongues (Acts 19:6).

In fact, the connection between spiritual gifts and the miraculous abilities described in Mark 16:17–18 is the key to parsing what Jesus said—and to understanding what's expected of each believer. Notice what Paul wrote to the Corinthians:

Now you are the body of Christ and individually members of it. And God has appointed in the church first apostles, second prophets, third teachers, then miracles, then gifts of healing, helping, administrating, and various kinds of tongues. Are all apostles? Are all prophets? Are all teachers? Do all work miracles? Do all possess gifts of healing? Do all speak with tongues? Do all interpret? (1 Cor 12:27-30)

Paul's questions here are rhetorical: By God's design, believers receive different spiritual gifts. If not all believers are given the gift of tongues—which Jesus mentions alongside exorcism in Mark 16:17-18—then we should not expect all believers to have the duty or giftedness to cast out demons. Jesus' words hint that the Spirit will empower those whom he chooses for such tasks. Threats against believers—spiritual or physical—do not impede the advance of Christ's kingdom.

43

The Word Was God

"In the beginning was the Word, and the Word was with God, and the Word was God." John 1:1 is, by far, one of the most familiar verses in the Bible. We know "the Word" speaks of Jesus (John 1:14), but where did John get the idea that "the Word" could refer to God as a person?

The answer lies partly in the translation John used. While John used the Greek word *logos* when referring to "the Word," he himself was likely influenced by Aramaic translations of the Old Testament.[1] In Jesus' day, Aramaic was the Jewish people's native language. While the Old Testament was translated from the Hebrew into Greek, the language of the wider Gentile world, it was also translated into Aramaic. These Aramaic translations are called Targums. One specific Targum of the Pentateuch, Targum Onqelos, was sanctioned by Jewish religious authorities for use in the synagogue.[2]

The Targums telegraph the idea of God as "Word" in many places—in vivid, sometimes startling ways. Many Jews of John's day would have been familiar with the idea. The Aramaic term for "word," *memra*, was often used as another way to refer to God. Consider Numbers 14:11 in the ESV and from Targum Neofiti, noting the words in bold:[3]

English Standard Version	Targum Neofiti
And the LORD said to Moses, "How long will this people despise me? And how long **will they not believe** **in me,** in spite of all **the signs** that **I** have **done** among **them**?"	And the LORD said to Moses, "How long **will they not believe** **in** the name of **my Word** in spite of all **the signs** of my miracles that **I** have **done** among **them**?"

In the Targum rendering, the LORD refers to himself as "my Word," using the Aramaic term *memra*. John calls Jesus "the Word made flesh" in John 1:14, possibly alluding to Numbers 14:11. He does this because the translations he had heard so many times in the synagogue had taught him that God was the Word—the *memra*—and he believed Jesus was God. John even echoes the Targum's version of Numbers 14:11 later on:

> When Jesus had said these things, he departed and hid himself from them. Though **he** had **done** so many **signs** before **them**, **they** still did **not believe in him.** (John 12:36–37)

Memra is used hundreds of times in the Targums to describe God, often in passages where the language presumes God is present in physical, human form: "And they heard the sound of the *memra* of the Lord God walking in the garden" (Targum Neofiti Gen 3:8).[4]

Because of the Targums, Jews in the days of Jesus and John would have understood the notion that God could come to them in human form. John believed that was exactly what he and the disciples had witnessed in Jesus, so it was natural for him to refer to Jesus as the Word. John wrote his gospel in Greek, but his theology was Jewish, conveyed to him through Aramaic. Therefore, both Jews and non-Jewish people got the point in unmistakable terms: The Word of the Old Testament had been made flesh (John 1:14) and walked among us.

44

The Table of Nations and Acts 2

Millions of Christians each year remember the day of Pentecost on the church calendar. Although Pentecost is one of the more familiar passages in the New Testament outside the Gospels, the Old Testament context of Acts 2 is largely unknown.

Overview

The Old Testament backdrop for the events of Acts 2 is the Table of Nations in Genesis 10 and its relationship to Deuteronomy 32:8-9.[1] The Deuteronomy passage alludes to Yahweh's dispersal of the nations at Babel and describes his *disinheriting* or rejecting those nations. According to Deuteronomy 32:8-9 (and its parallel, Deut 4:19-20) Yahweh, the God of Israel, removed the nations from direct relationship with himself and gave them over to the administration of other, lesser gods (*elohim*). From that point forward, Yahweh would be in direct relationship exclusively with Israel:

> When the Most High apportioned the nations as an inheritance, when he divided up humankind, he established the borders of the peoples according to

the number of the sons of God. But Yahweh's portion is his people, Jacob his allotted inheritance. (Deut 32:8–9)[2]

Many English translations—based on the traditional Hebrew text of the Old Testament—read "sons of Israel" or "children of Israel" here instead of "sons of God." The phrase "sons of God" is drawn from manuscripts of Deuteronomy 32 found among the Dead Sea Scrolls—scrolls much older than the traditional "received" text.[3]

Deuteronomy 32:8–9 is fundamental for understanding the worldview of Old Testament Israel. These two verses reveal the existence of the foreign divine beings and assert their inferiority to Yahweh. Israelites, in other words, believed that Yahweh, their own supreme, unique God, sentenced the nations and their gods to each other. At Babel, God, like a father dismissing and disinheriting his children, judges all the nations for their disobedience (Gen 11:1–9). Then, in the very next chapter, he calls Abraham (Gen 12:1–3), in effect starting over to create an earthly human family for himself. The rest of the Old Testament assumes Israel's unique relationship to Yahweh. Eventually, however, Israel's unfaithfulness led Yahweh to scattered the people among the other nations—effectively dismissing them in a manner reminiscent of the nations at Babel. But God did not simply undo his plans—Israel and its people were to be the conduit through whom Yahweh would progressively reclaim all the Gentile nations, a movement we know as the church—which in turn would bring Jews (Israelites) back to God.

Acts 2, the Tower of Babel, and the Table of Nations

Consider Acts 2 against the backdrop of this worldview:

> When the day of Pentecost arrived, they were all together in one place. ² And suddenly there came from heaven a sound like a mighty rushing wind, and it filled the entire house where they were sitting. ³ And **divided** [*diamerizo*] tongues as of fire appeared to them and rested on each one of them. ⁴ And they were all filled with the Holy Spirit and began to speak in other tongues as the Spirit gave them utterance. ⁵ Now there were dwelling in Jerusalem Jews, devout men from every nation under heaven. ⁶ And at this sound the multitude came together, and they were **bewildered** [*syncheō*], because each one was hearing them speak in his own language. ⁷ And they were amazed and astonished, saying, "Are not all these who are speaking Galileans? ⁸ And how is it that we hear, each of us in his own native language? ⁹ Parthians and Medes and Elamites and residents of Mesopotamia, Judea and Cappadocia, Pontus and Asia, ¹⁰ Phrygia and Pamphylia, Egypt and the parts of Libya belonging to Cyrene, and visitors from Rome, ¹¹ both Jews and proselytes, Cretans and Arabians— we hear them telling in our own tongues the mighty works of God." (Acts 2:1–11)

The two words in bold are crucial for understanding the underlying Old Testament significance of Acts 2 and the events of Pentecost. The Greek word *syncheō*, translated "bewildered," is used in the Septuagint version of the Tower of Babel story in Gen 11:7: "Come, and let us go down there to confound [*syncheō*] their language" (*LES*). Both Acts 2:6 and the Septuagint version of Genesis 11:7 link *syncheō* with confusion over human speech. In Genesis 11, of course, the context is the division of the nations (and their languages) at Babel. The other important Greek word in this passage from Acts is *diamerizō*, translated "divided." That term appears in the other major passage that refers to the events at Babel—the Septuagint of Deut 32:8:

> When the Most High distributed [*diamerizō*] nations,
> as he scattered the descendants of Adam, he set up
> boundaries for the nations according to the number
> of the angels of God. (*LES*)

These two terms are likely allusions to the story of Babel, so Luke is drawing on the Septuagint of Gen 11 and Deut 32 to connect the events of Acts 2 with the imagery of Babel and the Table of Nations. In Acts 2, Jews from around the known world were present in Jerusalem on Pentecost; many of them heard the good news in their native languages, a sign that the gospel was going to spread through these men, beginning at Jerusalem (compare Acts 1:8). The work of Jesus was thus going to overcome the division of humanity into many languages and nations at Babel.

Luke's list of nations in Acts 2, however, is perhaps the most startling aspect of the passage. Genesis 10 provides the context for understanding this list just as Gen 11 serves as the necessary background for the symbolic reversal of the confusion of language in Acts 2. The nations listed in Gen 10 represent the known world—a spreading out of humanity that resulted from God's dispersing in Gen 11. At the time Genesis 10 was written, the known world included Mesopotamia, the lands beyond it to the east, Asia Minor, the Levant (Syria and Canaan), Arabia, Egypt and North Africa, the areas of eastern Africa along the coast of the Red Sea, and a few other points around the Mediterranean Sea. Tarshish was the westernmost point of the known world.

While the places named in Acts 2 and in the Table of Nations from Genesis are different, the lists serve the same purpose—to outline the extent of the known world of their times. In Acts 1:8, the disciples are commissioned to take the gospel to the whole world—"You will be my witnesses in Jerusalem and in all Judea and Samaria, and to the end of the earth." In the first century AD, they likely thought of the end of civilization—the furthest extent of Roman rule—as the "end of the earth."

Through the events at Pentecost, three thousand Jews came to believe in Jesus (Acts 2:41); those converts returned to their homelands carrying the message of the gospel and furthering God's plan to reclaim the nations dispossessed at Babel.

45

Paul's Missionary Goals

The book of Acts ends in Rome with Paul imprisoned and ready to appeal to Caesar, but Rome does not represent the culmination of God's plan to reclaim the disinherited nations.[1] Genesis 10 lists one location farther west than Rome—in fact, it's the westernmost point in the list—Tarshish. Tarshish was a Phoenician colony on the southern coast of what would become Spain (*Spania*).[2] We know from Paul's letter to the Romans that he intended to go to Spain after his Roman imprisonment:[3]

> [24] I hope to see you in passing as I go to Spain, and to be helped on my journey there by you, once I have enjoyed your company for a while. ... [28] When therefore I have completed this and have delivered to them what has been collected, I will leave for Spain by way of you. (Rom 15:24, 28)

The early church father Clement reports that Paul did, indeed, reach "the limits of the west" as the culmination of his evangelistic journeys:

Paul pointed the way to the prize of endurance. Having borne chains seven times, having been exiled, having been stoned, having been a preacher in both the east and in the west, he received the noble fame of his faith. Having taught righteousness to the whole world and having come to **the limits of the west and having given his testimony before the rulers, thus he was set free from the world** and was taken up to the holy place, having become the greatest example of endurance.[4]

Only when Paul preached the gospel in Spain—reaching Tarshish, the westernmost part of the known world—would his life's mission be finished. Paul's mission as apostle to the Gentiles meant he was apostle to the disinherited nations; his drive to reach Spain suggests he was actually conscious that his missionary efforts for Jesus were part of a divine plan to reverse the disinheritance of those nations at Babel. Paul reveals this understanding in Romans 11:25 when he refers to "the fullness of the Gentiles" coming in. This phrase is an allusion to Old Testament passages describing the nations as one day returning to worship Yahweh (e.g., Isa 2:2–5; 11:10; 66:18–20; Mic 4:1–4).

> *Only when Paul preached the gospel in Spain—reaching Tarshish, the westernmost part of the known world—would his life's mission be finished.*

Throughout his letters, Paul quotes or alludes to the Old Testament to show that the long-promised day of salvation was happening now, during his lifetime. In the Old

Testament, the divine plan of Jewish belief in Jesus as Messiah was preceded by something Paul referred to as "the fullness of the Gentiles" (Rom 11:25). Paul makes it clear in Romans 9–11 that Gentile inclusion in the people of God was made possible by a temporary hardening of heart among the Jews (Rom 11:25–26). The key to undoing this hardening was to accomplish the mission of Gentile evangelism. Only then would Paul's passionate longing for his own Jewish brethren to believe in Jesus come to full fruition (Rom 9:3). Only then would the Deliverer (Jesus) come again from Zion (Rom 11:26). Once the "fullness of the Gentiles" comes in, "all Israel will be saved" (Rom 11:25–26). But how does the "fullness of the Gentiles" relate to Tarshish or Spain? Isaiah 66:18–20 prophesies that Yahweh would gather all nations to see his glory. To those nations, God would give a "sign" of his promised salvation. That sign would be delivered by survivors from the Jewish exile, sent by God into those far-off nations. The lands of Tarshish, Put, Lud, Tubal, and Javan are specifically mentioned. Those Jewish emissaries would declare Yahweh's glory among the nations, and the conversion of the Gentiles would also bring the Jews in all those nations to return to worship Yahweh. Paul likely believed the "sign" was Jesus (compare Isa 7:14). Paul knew well that the conversion process of Jewish exiles began at Pentecost, where Jews from nations scattered throughout the Mediterranean saw the Spirit act on the disciples, heard the gospel, and believed. They returned to their own countries to spread the word to the Gentiles (see Acts 2).

The final missionary goal for Paul was Spain, the "end of the world" in popular thinking (Rom 15:24). This place appears in the list in Isaiah 66 since Spain is the location of

Tarshish (Isa 66:19). When Paul wrote Romans, he knew the gospel had spread to every region mentioned in Isaiah 66—except Tarshish. He believed that his mission, the fullness of the Gentiles, and the salvation of his Jewish brethren, would be fulfilled once he reached Spain.

46

Divine Misdirection

The cross is the central event of the Bible. Without the cross there is no redemption, no reversal of the human condition, no restoration of Eden in a new earth, and no defeat of evil. But how was it that intelligent evil powers—even Satan himself—didn't figure out what God was up to in sending Jesus? If Satan had discovered God's plan, he could have attempted to prevent evil powers from bringing Jesus to the cross. The powers of darkness wouldn't have needed to be stronger than God; they only needed to do *nothing*.

The powers of darkness wouldn't have needed to be stronger than God; they only needed to do nothing.

We read the Gospels with full hindsight. We can't imagine how the disciples missed what we see about the cross, but the Bible directly says they did. After the resurrection, they needed their minds opened to realize that the Messiah *had* to suffer, die, and rise again to bring salvation (Luke 24:44–47). But they weren't the only ones in the dark.

The Gospels give no indication that Satan or the demons knew what God's plan entailed. Demons certainly knew Jesus was the Son of God, but exactly how God's kingdom would be restored was a mystery hidden "in God" (Matt 4:3-6; 8:29; Eph 1:7-9; 3:3-11). If the disciples didn't know the plan, then we shouldn't expect that Satan or the demons would know it either. The powers of darkness are not omniscient—only God is all-knowing. The Apostle Paul explored this subject:

> Yet among the mature we do impart wisdom, although it is not a wisdom of this age or of the rulers of this age, who are doomed to pass away. But we impart a secret and hidden wisdom of God, which God decreed before the ages for our glory. None of the rulers of this age understood this, for if they had, they would not have crucified the Lord of glory. (1 Cor 2:6-8)

The key term here is *archontōn*, translated "rulers." This term was used widely in Greek literature to refer to human rulers. Paul uses it that way on occasion (e.g., Rom 13:3), but here he has spiritual powers in mind. We know this because he is discussing God himself in the previous verses.

Paul is drawing on his knowledge of the Old Testament. Deuteronomy 32:8-9[1] and Daniel 10 inform us that Israel was God's people, the lone nation aligned with him. The other nations were under spiritual powers as a result of God's punishment of the rebellion at the Tower of Babel, where the nations were divided (Gen 11:1-9). Deuteronomy 32:17 calls these divine beings "demons" (*shedim*). Daniel 10:13 uses the term "prince" (*sar*). Israel is watched over by the archangel Michael, and so he is called Israel's "prince" (Dan 10:21; 12:1). The Septuagint—the Greek translation of the Hebrew Bible frequently used by Paul—translates *sar* with the Greek term *archōn*.[2] Elsewhere Paul uses the related term *archē* to refer to these spiritual powers (Eph 6:12). The Gospels refer to Satan himself with this word (Mark 3:22; John 12:31; 14:30; 16:11).

From these passages, a picture emerges of the nations of the world under the dominion of dark powers hostile to God's plan. God kept his plan hidden for good reason. Had those dark powers known that manipulating people to kill Jesus would initiate the end of their own rule, they never would have done so.

God's plans are often full of mystery. But the cross—this mystery hidden in God—turned the tables on his evil opponents and turned the course of history. It's the type of sacrificial love that the dark powers never could have imagined.

47

Who is the God of This World?

We are creatures of habit. If we do something often enough, the "right way" of doing things comes to feel self-evident. The more we hear or read about an idea, the more "obvious" that thing becomes. But not everyone thinks the same way or sees the same thing. This carries over into Bible interpretation. Second Corinthians 4:3–4 is a case in point:

> And even if our gospel is veiled, it is veiled to those who are perishing. In their case the god of this world has blinded the minds of the unbelievers, to keep them from seeing the light of the gospel of the glory of Christ, who is the image of God.

Many of us would interpret the "god of this world" as a reference to Satan. After all, Paul mentions Satan in several other places in this letter (2 Cor 2:11; 11:14; 12:7). But not all interpreters agree.

Why God?

The question of just who is "the god of this world" is a very old one. The early church fathers Cyril of Jerusalem and Ambrosiaster believed Paul was talking about God himself. Their argument was quite straightforward. Only God is truly God of this world or age (the Greek word is *aiōn*, which can denote an age or era). God is the true God of every age. However, Cyril of Jerusalem and Ambrosiaster favored this interpretation for theological reasons. The Greek word for "god" is *theos*. If Satan is called *theos* in 2 Corinthians 4:4, then it seems to follow that, when Jesus is referred to as *theos* (Titus 1:3–4; John 1:1–3, 17–18), those verses aren't referring to him as the true God. Therefore, the early church fathers argued that we shouldn't see Satan as the "god of this world" in 2 Cor 4:4; we should interpret the phrase as referring to the one true God. At first it seems unthinkable that the true God would, as 2 Cor 4:3–4 says, blind the eyes of unbelievers from embracing Jesus. But elsewhere Paul says that specifically:

> Israel failed to obtain what it was seeking. The elect obtained it, but the rest were hardened, as it is written, "God gave them a spirit of stupor, eyes that would not see and ears that would not hear, down to this very day" … I do not want you to be unaware of this mystery, brothers: a partial hardening has come upon Israel, until the fullness of the Gentiles has come in. (Rom 11:7–8, 25; compare Isa 6:9–10)

But is this judgment, aimed at Israel, what Paul is talking about in 2 Cor 4:3–4? It doesn't seem so, since the comment refers generally to unbelievers in the present age. And that inconsistency is a good reason to reconsider Satan as the god of this world.

Why Satan?

If we look at Paul's use of the word "god" (*theos*), we find it isn't unprecedented for him to use that word to refer to something other than the true God. In Philippians 3:19 Paul says of Jesus' enemies, "their god (*theos*) is their belly." Paul uses the term *theos* to speak of that thing which has controlling power over a person. Also, in 1 Corinthians 8:5, Paul acknowledges that pagans offer sacrifices to other gods (*theoi*), entities he later refers to as demons (1 Cor 10:19–20).

Paul uses that language because it comes from the Old Testament (Deut 32:17). He also echoes New Testament descriptions of Satan as the "ruler of this world (*kosmos*)" (John 12:31; 14:30; 16:11):

> And you were dead in the trespasses and sins in which you once walked, following the course of this world, following the prince of the power of the air, the spirit that is now at work in the sons of disobedience. (Eph 2:1–2)

The context of Ephesians 2:1–2 is similar to that of 2 Cor 3–4: It explains why people do not believe the gospel and even oppose it. Since Paul's use of *theos* in Phil 3:19 shows us the term could be used to speak of controlling a dominion, Satan could easily be described with that term because he rules over unbelievers.

Darkness and Blindness

There are other contextual clues. The theme of being "in darkness"—a corollary to being spiritually blinded—is specifically associated with Satan and demonic powers

(Acts 26:18; Eph 6:12). In addition, spiritual blindness is referred to dozens of times in the New Testament (Eph 5:8, 11; Col 1:13; 1 John 2:11). This is ultimately what makes Satan the better candidate for the "god of this world."

After using the phrase "god of this world," Paul says in 2 Corinthians 4:6:

> For God, who said, "Let light shine out of darkness," has shone in our hearts to give the light of the knowledge of the glory of God in the face of Jesus Christ.

Paul contrasts darkness—and hence blindness—with both the glory of God and the person of Jesus. If God himself were the one doing the blinding in this passage, that contrast would make little sense.

Disagreements in biblical interpretation are inevitable. Nothing in the context of the Old Testament prevents the conclusion that the "god of this world" is Satan. Some thinkers in the early church, however, saw things differently.

48

New Testament Language of
Spiritual Adoption and Sonship

New Testament writers used the language of divine sonship to describe believers in Jesus. Similarly, the Church, the community carrying on God's revived kingdom rule on earth, was associated with Israel, God's earlier kingdom community. Since many believers were Gentiles and not part of the original human family of God (meaning Israel), New Testament writers also described attaining membership as children in God's family as "adoption." The New Testament children of God, believers in Jesus, are the spiritual seed of Abraham (Gal 3:7–9, 25–29).

The Old Testament Context

The Old Testament writers use the language of divine sonship in two contexts: referring to heavenly beings, the "sons of God" (Job 1:6; 2:1; 38:7; Gen 6:2, 4; Deut 32:8; Ps 89:6), and referring to human beings, specifically, members of the nation of Israel (Exod 4:22–23; Deut 14:1; Isa 1:2; Jer 31:9; Hos 1:10). The Israelite king, as the representative of the nation, is also described as a son of God (Pss 2:7; 89:27).

In the Old Testament, God's heavenly dwelling was also his headquarters, the place where he met with his council, the members of the heavenly host who served him in the administration of his creation. This is the context for the plural language of Gen 1:26. God created human beings to reflect his image (i.e., represent him) just as the members of his heavenly host did. Heaven would be on earth, administered by all God's imagers.

The fall disrupted this relationship. Though God promised Eve a human descendant who would undo the effects of sin and restore the relationship between God and his children (Gen 3:15), the early chapters of the Old Testament reveal human resistance to God's rule. God eventually responded by dispersing the people at Babel (Gen 11:1–9), effectually disinheriting them and placing them under the administration of the lesser sons of God or divine council (Deut 32:8–9; compare Deut 4:19–20).[1] This act was a punishment for their rebellion, but the rejection of the nations would not be permanent. God chose to work through Abram and his offspring to raise up new children of God who would restore his rule on earth and be the means of blessing to the disinherited nations (Gen 12:1–3). This was "the gospel spoken to Abraham" (Gal 3:8), delivered by Jesus himself as the pre-incarnate Word of God (Gen 15:1; John 1:1–3, 14; 8:56).

The rest of the Old Testament focuses on God's chosen people, the offspring of Abraham, later called Israel, and their interactions with the other nations. The Israelites were commanded to avoid intermarriage with these other nations and to reject the worship of their national gods (Deut 7:3–5). The Old Testament story of Israel, however, is dominated by their failure to follow these commands—regularly worshiping foreign gods and eventually suffering the punishment of exile (2 Kgs 24–25). God's plan to redeem his people from this punishment centered on the arrival of a single human offspring out of Israel, a son of Eve, a member of the line of David, God's chosen king, to bring everything full circle. This person is Jesus.

New Testament Re-Purposing of Divine Sonship Language

In view of the Old Testament context, it is no surprise that the New Testament writers utilized the language of divine sonship for believers in Jesus.[2] They also associated the Church, the community carrying on God's revived kingdom rule on earth, with Israel, God's earlier kingdom community, but since many believers were Gentiles—not a part of the people of Israel by birth—New Testament writers also used terms like "adoption" to describe membership as children in God's family. Believers in Jesus are the spiritual seed of Abraham. Paul states this explicitly in Gal 3:7–9 (see also Gal 3:25–29).

The language of divine inheritance advances the Old Testament idea that humans were meant to be in the family of God. The New Testament writers thought in terms of "adoption," "heir," and "inheritance" to describe what the Church really is—the reestablished human family of God. They also used these terms to describe what the Church will be in the final form of the kingdom on the new earth when believers are glorified. The believer's destiny is to become what Adam and Eve originally were in Eden in God's presence before the Fall: immortal, glorified imagers of God (see 2 Pet 1:2–4).

49

The Lord, Who Is the Spirit

It was Peter who said of Paul's writings, "There are some things in them that are hard to understand" (2 Pet 3:16). One thing Peter might have been talking about is Paul's statement in Ephesians 4:8, which has long puzzled Bible students. To understand Paul's logic, we need to begin with Psalm 68:18, the passage he draws on in this verse:

Psalm 68:18	Ephesians 4:8
You ascended on high, leading a host of captives in your train and receiving gifts among men.	Therefore it says, "When he ascended on high he led a host of captives, and he gave gifts to men."

The "ascent on high" in Psalm 68 referred to a mountain—Mount Bashan (Ps 68:15). In the Old Testament, Bashan was a region associated with spiritual evil, the quasi-divine, giant Rephaim (Deut 1:4; 3:10–11; Josh 9:10; 12:4–5).[1] God desired this mountain for his own dwelling (Ps 68:16)—he wanted its evil powers defeated. For Paul, Jesus is the fulfillment of Psalm 68. Jesus defeated the powers of darkness when he died and rose again (1 Pet 3:22; Eph 1:20–21; Col 2:15).

It's important to recognize that both passages are describing a conquest, not a rescue. In Psalm 68 the victorious captain of the army leads the enemy captives. Many commentators assume that Ephesians 4:8 describes captives being liberated. That isn't the case. There is no liberation; there is conquest. The passages agree in this respect. While we can understand Jesus' crucifixion and resurrection as the conquest of sin, evil, and death itself, a key difference between these texts complicates the comparison. In Psalm 68, God *receives* gifts after his victory, but Ephesians 4 describes Jesus *giving* gifts. How does this make any sense?

Paul's wording points to the result of Jesus' conquest. In the ancient world, a conqueror would parade the captives and demand tribute for himself. But booty also was distributed after a conquest. Paul knew that. He quotes Psalm 68:18 to explain that after Jesus conquered his demonic enemies by his resurrection, he distributed the benefits to his believing Church: apostles, prophets, evangelists, pastors, and teachers (Eph 4:11). How is Paul getting this idea? He explains himself in Ephesians 4:9–12:

> In saying, "He ascended," what does it mean but that he had also descended into the lower regions, the earth? He who descended is the one who also ascended far above all the heavens, that he might fill all things.) And he gave the apostles, the prophets, the evangelists, the shepherds and teachers, to equip the saints for the work of ministry, for building up the body of Christ.

Paul argues that Jesus' conquering resurrection ascent was followed by a descent that led to gifts for the Church. There are two possible explanations for this descent. The most common view is that "the lower regions of the earth" (LEB) into which Jesus descended refers to the grave, the realm of the dead. This is possible, since the same idea appears in 1 Peter 3:18–22.

However, another approach is more likely. Instead of saying "of the earth" in verse 9, the ESV inserts a comma. The interpretive effect is that Jesus descended to "the lower regions, [i.e.,] the earth." This option better fits the context, because the gifts are given to living believers who are on earth. If this is correct, then the descent refers not to Jesus' time in the grave, but rather to the Holy Spirit being poured out on earth on the day of Pentecost.

While many passages clarify that Jesus and the Spirit are different persons (e.g., Jesus' baptism: Matt 3:16; Jesus' temptation: 4:1; the Great Commission: 28:18–20), the New Testament also identifies the Spirit with Jesus in a half-dozen passages (such as Acts 16:6–7: "[Paul, Silas, and Timothy were] prevented by the Holy Spirit from speaking the message in Asia. ... [T]he Spirit of Jesus did not permit them" [LEB]).[2]

Paul's point is profound: The resurrection of Jesus and the coming of the Spirit are two sides of the same coin. Believers benefit from both. As Paul wrote elsewhere, "The Lord is the Spirit, and where the Spirit of the Lord is, there is freedom" (2 Cor 3:17).

50

Paul, Puppies, and People with Tattoos

We love the letter of Philippians for its uplifting, faith-affirming tone. Although Paul wrote it in prison, it resonates joy. Paul's circumstances didn't put him in a bad mood. But something else did. He writes:

> Finally, my brothers, rejoice in the Lord. To write the same things to you is no trouble to me and is safe for you. Look out for the dogs, look out for the evildoers, look out for those who mutilate the flesh. For we are the circumcision, who worship by the Spirit of God and glory in Christ Jesus and put no confidence in the flesh. (Phil 3:1–3)

We have no trouble understanding Paul when he says, "Look out for the evildoers." But dogs? People who mutilate the flesh? Did Paul hate puppies and people with tattoos? Not exactly. Like any statement in the Bible, this one requires context to help us get inside the writer's head.

Dogs in the Ancient World

In the ancient world (except in the Egyptian and Phoenician cultures), dogs were routinely despised. Their instinctive, base behavior—such as eating dead, decayed flesh or consuming their own vomit—disgusted ancient people (Exod 22:31; 1 Kgs 14:11; Prov 26:11). The appropriate insult to heap on someone you considered worthless was "dead dog" (2 Sam 16:9; see also Deut 23:17–18).

Paul, with his thorough knowledge of the Old Testament, would have been acquainted with the use of the term in the Bible and in his culture. The label makes sense here since Paul follows it by warning "look out for the evildoers." Paul didn't hate puppies. He hated evil.

Mutilators of the Flesh

But what about "those who mutilate the flesh"? What sense can we make of that? As odd as it sounds, this phrase is one of the keys to understanding just who Paul is referring to in Philippians 3.

The phrase literally reads "look out for the mutilation." The Greek word behind "mutilation" is the noun *katatomē*. Paul likely chose it deliberately because it sounds a bit like another Greek word—*peritomē*, which means "circumcision." Right after Paul warns the Philippians to "look out for the mutilation," he adds an explanation: "For we are the circumcision, who worship by the Spirit of God and glory in Christ Jesus and put no confidence in the flesh" (Phil 3:3). Paul was using a satirical play on words to make his point.

Paul wasn't objecting to circumcision itself. He never characterizes circumcision as something to be abhorred (Rom 3:1–2; 1 Cor 7:18). Paul was objecting to those who taught that circumcision was essential for salvation—for inclusion in the community of believers.

The idea that any ritual could result in salvation or merit God's favor was incompatible with salvation by grace through faith. Gentiles who believed according to the faith of Abraham were "blessed along with Abraham" (Gal 3:9), because "in Christ Jesus you are all sons of God, through faith" (Gal 3:26). Whether Jew or Gentile, those who believe in Jesus are the spiritual children of Abraham; they are heirs to the promises God made to him (Gal 3:29). His opponents' perversion of the gospel infuriated Paul. Using the term "mutilation" was his sarcastic way of showing contempt for the false teaching.

Paul's derogatory terms for his opponents weren't cast out lightly. They were born out of a deep concern for the gospel message: we cannot merit salvation, nor can we earn grace. Salvation comes through faith in the grace God showed us through Jesus' work on the cross.

51

Watch Your Language!

One of the most frequently repeated maxims about translation, including Bible translation, is that "every translator is a traitor." The point of this saying is not that translations are unreliable—it's that they aren't perfect. Every translation loses something of the original meaning. In most cases this is inadvertent, but sometimes it's deliberate, as in Philippians 3:8:

> Indeed, I count everything as loss because of the surpassing worth of knowing Christ Jesus my Lord. For his sake I have suffered the loss of all things and count them as rubbish, in order that I may gain Christ.

The verse might sound straightforward, but the translator has softened what was likely its intended force. The Greek word translated "rubbish" is *skybalon*; while the term appears only here in the New Testament, it is found in classical Greek literature as a word for human excrement or manure.[1]

Why So Crass?

Paul also uses rough—even crude—language elsewhere in his writings. For example, in Galatians, Paul's primary opponents are Jews (or Jewish Christians) insisting that Gentile converts practice certain parts of the Mosaic law to ensure their inclusion in the people of God. One such element was circumcision. Paul gets so exasperated that at one point he wishes the people insisting on circumcision would just castrate themselves (Gal 5:11-12). And Paul is not the first or only biblical writer to use such strong language.

> *Paul uses rough—even crude—language in his writings.*

The Precedent for Euphemism

It would be misguided to view the translators' choice of "rubbish" over "excrement" in Phil 3:8 as dishonest. While it's true that the term is in the text, the translator shows sensitivity to propriety and the expectations of "polite society." In seeking to soften offensive language, the translator follows the lead of the biblical writers themselves.

The Old Testament writers were especially adept at using euphemisms in place of scatological language—terms associated with certain bodily functions and their corresponding body parts. For example, Zechariah 3:3-4 speaks of the high priest's garments as being "filthy" (*tso'i*). The Hebrew word is literally "what goes out," a euphemistic reference to excrement. Thus, Zechariah depicts Joshua the high priest as one who has soiled himself and now stands before God. The imagery is repulsive—but that's the point:

Sin is repulsive. Modern translators have to decide whether to use biblical euphemisms or opt for new substitutions.

Paul's Point

To understand why Paul used coarse language in Philippians 3:8, we need to look at what he was calling "rubbish." In Philippians 3:4–7, Paul lists all the things that he had presumed made him acceptable to God: his circumcision, his zeal for the Mosaic law, his previous status as a Pharisee, and his efforts to snuff out Christianity. He now considers all of these things as excrement—something not only viscerally offensive, but ceremonially unclean for sacred space in the old tabernacle and temple (Deut 23:12–14; Ezek 4:12–13). Paul could not have chosen a more vivid way of communicating his point that, next to Christ's work on the cross, none of those things mattered to God.

Shock and Awe with a Purpose

The Bible is not a prudish book. Paul at times resorted to earthy language to jolt his audience to attention and to punctuate the seriousness of his teaching. Isaiah and Ezekiel did the same thing. Yet Scripture also demonstrates that thoughtless, flippant crudity is no virtue (Eph 5:4; Phil 4:8). The Bible provides a model of transparency without indecency that's worth imitating.

52

No Longer Slaves

The church at Colossae—with both moral and doctrinal problems—was like any other fledgling congregation to which Paul ministered. One example of the church's doctrinal problems that has received considerable attention among Bible scholars has been labeled the "Colossian heresy." Two passages are of central importance to understanding this heresy and how Paul addresses it:

> See to it that no one takes you captive by philosophy and empty deceit, according to human tradition, according to the elemental spirits (*stoicheia*) of the world, and not according to Christ. (Col 2:8)

> Let no one disqualify you, insisting on asceticism and worship of angels. ... If with Christ you died to the elemental spirits (*stoicheia*) of the world, why, as if you were still alive in the world, do you submit to regulations—"Do not handle, Do not taste, Do not touch." (Col 2:18, 20–21)

In both passages, Paul uses a Greek term—*stoicheia*—that is simultaneously well understood by scholars but mystifying in terms of what Paul is thinking when he employs it. The term *stoicheia* occurs widely in Greek literature to describe (1) basic principles of religious teaching (e.g., rules, rituals); (2) rudimentary substances of the physical world (earth, wind, fire, water); (3) astral deities (the notion that celestial objects were divine beings); and (4) spiritual beings in general.[1]

References to *stoicheia* occur seven times in the New Testament. The only instance that seems certain with respect to meaning is Hebrews 5:12, where *stoicheia* describes the law ("basic principles of the oracles of God"). When it comes to Paul's use of the term (Col 2:8, 20; and Gal 4:3, 9), there is no consensus among scholars as to his meaning. The general context of Paul's discussion in Galatians 4 and Colossians 2 includes spiritual forces—angels, principalities and powers, false gods—which suggests *stoicheia* may refer to such beings. He is certainly contrasting *stoicheia* with salvation in Christ in some way. Since Paul is speaking to both Jews and Gentiles, he might be using the term in different ways with respect to each audience. With a Jewish audience in view in Galatians 4:1-7, Paul's use of *stoicheia* in 4:3 likely refers to the law and religious teaching (similar to Heb 5:12). But in 4:8-11, where the audience shifts to Gentiles, it seems coherent to see *stoicheia* in 4:9 as referring to spiritual beings—probably astral deities (the "Fates"). The reference to "times and seasons and years" (4:10) would therefore point to astrological beliefs, not the Jewish calendar. Paul is therefore denying the idea that the celestial objects (sun, moon, stars) are deities. His Gentile readers should not be enslaved by the idea that these objects controlled their destiny.

In terms of the "Colossian heresy," both Jews and Gentiles are likely in view; hence the term *stoicheia* would have had meaning for both audiences. Paul links what he says about *stoicheia* to the "worship of angels" (Col 2:18). Given that Paul and other New Testament writers have the Jewish law dispensed by angels (Gal 3:19; Acts 7:53; Heb 2:2), some scholars argue that, for

> *Believers in Christ are no longer enslaved to spiritual forces of any kind.*

Jewish readers, the *stoicheia* of Colossians may refer to a heresy that enslaved Jews to the law—including flawed worship of the angels associated with delivering the law to Israel. For Gentiles, these "angels" and the ascetic "regulations" of Colossians 2:20-21 may speak to a heretical emphasis on keeping in sync with pagan rituals and celestial divinities, who were thought to be angered when those rituals were neglected.

Whatever the ultimate, precise meaning, the contrast with the gospel of grace was crystal clear. Believers in Christ are no longer enslaved to spiritual forces of any kind. Legal demands and ritual obligations have been nailed to the cross (Col 2:14), resulting in forgiveness and freedom.

53

The Relationship of Baptism and Circumcision

Baptism is a controversial doctrine. Many Christian denominations say something distinctive about baptism, often in contradiction to each other. Some connect baptism to the removal of original sin, while others deny it has any connection to sin at all. Some believe it is a religious rite that sets recipient infants on their way to seeking God, while others reject baptizing infants. Some teach that it is a sign of a covenantal guarantee of election for the recipient, while others say it is a sign of conversion that has already taken place. Colossians 2:11–12 may point us to a greater understanding of baptism in biblical theology.

> In [Christ] also you were circumcised with a circumcision made without hands, by putting off the body of the flesh, by the circumcision of Christ, having been buried with him in baptism, in which you were also raised with him through faith in the powerful working of God, who raised him from the dead.

This passage forms a connection between baptism and circumcision. Though Paul doesn't specifically identify what that connection is, his words direct us to circumcision as an analogy. What we say about the meaning of baptism ought to be consistent with the meaning of circumcision.

What Circumcision Did Not Mean or Accomplish

Several aspects are clear in regard to circumcision in Old Testament theology and in the historical context of biblical Israel. The Old Testament story indicates that circumcision neither provided nor ensured salvation, nor did it lessen anyone's sinful impulse. In the Old Testament, most circumcised Israelites still turned away from God, practicing idolatry—their actions eventually prompting Yahweh to punish them with exile. The fact that Israelite men were circumcised meant nothing with respect to their spiritual inclination or destiny.

Though Paul doesn't specifically identify what that connection is, his words direct us to circumcision as an analogy.

Furthermore, the Old Testament texts are clear that circumcision was not practiced on women. While some cultures and religions around the world have practiced female circumcision, Israel only circumcised males.[1] This indicates that the cutting rite itself did nothing with respect to an individual's ultimate spiritual destiny—if it did, women would not have been excluded. Additionally, historical sources indicate that cultures other than Israel, such as Egypt, also practiced circumcision for men.[2] This shows that the rite itself had no efficacy in regard to salvation. Rather, its importance was in what the rite signified in conjunction with the promises God gave to Abraham and his descendants. The actual ritual of circumcision therefore had nothing to do with salvation or expressing faith in the God of Israel.

The Meaning of Circumcision

For all Israelites, circumcision was a physical, visible reminder of their identity as Yahweh's covenant people (Gen 17:1–14). They owed their existence both individually and corporately to a supernatural act of God on behalf of Abraham and Sarah in fulfillment of his covenant promise (Gen 17:15–21). Circumcision was a constant reminder of the supernatural grace of God.

For males, circumcision granted the recipient admission into the community of Israel—the community that had the exclusive truth of the true God. This truth included Yahweh's covenant relationship with Israel and their need to have "circumcised hearts" (i.e., to believe in Yahweh's promises and worship him alone; Deut 10:16; 30:6). In ancient patriarchal Israel, women were members of the community through marriage to a circumcised man or by being born to Israelite parents. Intermarriage with foreign men (i.e., uncircumcised so not part of Yahweh's covenant community) was forbidden, a prohibition that maintained the purity of the membership (Deut 7:35). This purity was directly related to the spiritual significance of circumcision.

Membership in the community was important for a specific reason: only this community had the truth—the "the oracles of God," as Paul called God's revelation to Israel (Rom 3:2). Only Israel had the truth in regard to the nature of the true God among all gods and how people could be rightly related to him (i.e., the way of salvation). Yahweh had created this human community with the goal of giving the way of salvation. This exclusivity is what is meant in Old Testament theology to be "elect" or "chosen" (Deut 7:7). Election was not equated with salvation since vast multitudes of elect Israelites were not saved due to their unfaithfulness. Every Israelite member of the exclusive community had to believe in the covenant promises and worship Yahweh. Circumcision meant access to this truth.

Circumcision as an Analogy to Baptism

The meaning and significance of circumcision connects to baptism in several aspects, whether one's position includes baptism of infants or not. Baptizing an infant makes that infant a member in the believing community, a local church. Hopefully, that church will teach the words of God and the way of salvation so that the child will hear the gospel and believe. The hope would be the same for an adult recipient of baptism. When Abraham and his entire household (even servants) were circumcised, the account does not identify who believed in Abraham's God and who did not. The assumption is that, as members of his household who would observe God's blessing and Abraham's faithfulness, they too would believe. Many adults who are baptized today have already made a faith decision—a type of baptism also described in the New Testament. When New Testament believers were baptized, they became members of the believing community. Such membership meant they regularly experienced community with other believers, something that would sustain their faith and help them to be assured of God's promises. This is equally true today. Membership in the family of God should both foster and sustain faith. These were God's same goals for Old Testament Israel.

54

Disarming the Powers of Darkness

Christians often talk about dark spiritual forces working against them in a range of situations, from disagreements with a neighbor to claims of demonic possession. Sadly, the way the New Testament portrays spiritual conflict is all too often neglected.

While Paul and other writers are clear that the war against sinister powers of darkness is ongoing, those same powers are routinely said to have been defeated by the cross. This crucial element of how we need to think about cosmic evil is evidenced in Colossians 2:15:

> When he had disarmed the rulers and the authorities, he made a display of them in public, triumphing over them by it.[1] (LEB)

Although this passage looks fairly straightforward, it has long puzzled interpreters for several reasons. The wording is similar to other passages, but it also differs significantly from those passages. For example, in Ephesians 4:8–10, Jesus "ascended on high" leading a line of captives in his wake. But in Colossians 2:15, Jesus isn't leading captives; rather, they are disarmed, publicly humiliated, and defeated, but apparently still working against him and us. Elsewhere, Paul has Christ leading believers in a "triumphal procession" (2 Cor 2:14). Are these passages mutually contradictory? Who are the "rulers and authorities"? If they weren't destroyed, what does Paul's description of what happened to them because of the cross mean?

In Ephesians 4, Paul is talking about demonic entities—the "bulls of Bashan" (Ps 22:12), the unholy mountain God wanted conquered in Psalm 68 (from which Paul quotes in Eph 4:8–10).[2] That mountain was associated with "prince Baal" (*baal-zebul*) in the Old Testament, the Canaanites' lord of the dead, and a template for Satan in the New Testament. Paul is trying to communicate Christ's victory over death at the cross and the binding (note the "prisoner" language) of Satan in terms of "legal ownership" over the souls of humanity. But Paul's perspective is a bit different in Colossians 2:15. The cross accomplished something different with respect to the "rulers and authorities" that Paul has in view here.

The three verbs Paul uses in Colossians 2:15 are *apekduomai* ("disarm"), *deigmatizō* ("put to shame" or "make a public display of"), and *thriambeuō* ("triumph over"). These Greek words are not common. Taken together, they refer to a public humiliation, a stripping of authority, or a loss of status and office—but not imprisonment or death. This is why scholars have noted the lack of a clear warfare parallel to the language.

The key to discerning Paul's meaning is his "rulers and authorities" reference. These terms are part of Paul's stock vocabulary for powers of darkness in the spiritual realm ("heavenly places"; Eph 3:10; 6:12). These terms are often used in tandem with others, such as "thrones" and "dominions" (Eph 1:21; Col 1:16). They are all labels for geographical dominion by spiritual powers. They reflect the cosmic-geographical supernatural worldview inherited by Paul from the Old Testament, where the gods "allotted" by Yahweh to the nations in punishment at Babel (Gen 11:1–9; Deut 32:8–9; Dan 10:13) turned away from him and seduced the Israelites (Deut 4:19–20; 17:2–3; 29:24–26; 32:17; Ps 82).[3]

> *Because of the cross, the spiritual beings hostile to Yahweh have lost—and are still losing—their status and rank over the nations as the kingdom of Christ expands over the world.*

Because of the cross, these hostile spiritual beings have lost—and are still losing—their status and rank over the nations as the kingdom of Christ expands over the world. They ultimately will be replaced by forgiven believers (Rev 2:25–27) who will "judge angels" (1 Cor 6:3), having become the new, glorified children of God at the end of the age (John 1:12; 1 John 3:1–3; Rom 8:18–19).

55

Inspiration Was a Process, Not an Event

Because the Bible says quite clearly that Scripture is "God-breathed" (2 Tim 3:16), Christians tend to think of inspiration as some sort of otherworldly event. In the course of many years of teaching biblical studies (and chatting with people at church), I've heard some pretty strange explanations of inspiration—about how God took control of the hand and mind of the writer, or how the authors slipped into a heaven-sent trance state, or how the Spirit whispered the precise words into their minds (or maybe just "impressed" them into their consciousness). Frankly, all of that sounds more like an episode of *The X-Files* than biblical theology. And it absolutely doesn't reflect what we actually find in Scripture about inspiration.

There are some transparent examples of why the "paranormal event" view of inspiration makes no sense. There are four gospels in the New Testament. Three of them (Matthew, Mark, and Luke) overlap with respect to the events they include about the life of Jesus, but those events may be dissimilar in the level of detail[1] or arranged in a different sequence.[2] Dialogue within shared episodes also diverges in vocabulary, length of statements, and who speaks

when. And even when the dialogue (in English translations) appears identical, it isn't. In the Greek text writers
can use different words, verb tenses, noun cases, conjunc-
tions, and so on. If the stories of Jesus were "whispered" to
the writers or downloaded into their semiconscious minds,
divergences like these are the last thing we should expect.
Would the Holy Spirit really want to yank our theological
chains like that? I doubt it.

There are a lot of other phenomena in the biblical text
that tell the careful reader quite clearly that inspiration
wasn't an event. Most biblical books show signs of edit-
ing. One of the best examples is the first four verses of the
book of Ezekiel:

> In the thirtieth year, in the fourth month, on the fifth
> day of the month, as **I was** among the exiles by the
> Chebar canal, the heavens were opened, and **I saw**
> visions of God. On the fifth day of the month (it was
> the fifth year of the exile of King Jehoiachin), the
> word of the LORD <u>came to Ezekiel</u> the priest, the son
> of Buzi, in the land of the Chaldeans by the Chebar
> canal, and the hand of the LORD was <u>upon him</u> there.
> As **I looked**, behold, a stormy wind came out of the
> north. (Ezek 1:1–4)

The first verse uses the first person in two instances—
indicated in bold. The first person language creates the
expectation that Ezekiel is writing about himself. But in
verse three there is a switch to the third person—indicated by underlining. Now the writer is clearly not Ezekiel, but is an anonymous author referring to Ezekiel in
the third person. Verse four switches back to first person

(in bold again). These switches are the tell-tale signs of an editor. The Holy Spirit is not suffering from schizophrenia. This material is clearly not dictated or downloaded or automated.

Instruments or Puppets?

While God does speak to people in Scripture, the passages that describe how biblical authors produced their texts never cast it in anomalous terms. According to the Bible, Scripture is the result of divine influence and the very normal human activity of speaking and, by extension, writing (2 Tim 3:16; 2 Pet 1:16–21). Writers report events and record feelings. They build arguments. They express themselves in poetry. They use sources. They borrow thoughts. They (or other hands that follow) rewrite and refine what was written. Authors are sensitive to genre, structure, literary devices, word choice, poetic parallelism, and narrative art. There is wordplay, irony, and premeditated structuring of plot. The books we have in our Bible are the result of work and careful thought. Biblical books were not slapped together. No part of any biblical book just "happened" out of the blue.

> *The books we have in our Bible are the result of work and careful thought. Biblical books were not slapped together.*

God's role is no less significant and intentional. God chose a wide range of people and providentially prepared them for the moment he would prompt them, either by his Spirit or by someone else's influence, to write something down for the benefit of God's people (or to collect and edit material from a prophetic figure). God put them in situations that would lead to the need for them to write the message God wanted preserved. He didn't need to put them into a trance and manipulate their fingers. They didn't need hand-holding (or mind control). They were his instruments, not his puppets.

Embracing the Bible's Humanity

Why does any of this matter? Because minimizing (or denying) the humanity behind biblical authorship is a surefire way to undermine the doctrine of inspiration. Explaining the Bible as something dispensed from a super-intelligent deity from out of the ether is irreconcilable with what we see in it. On the other hand, defining inspiration as a long process guided unfailingly by Providence helps account for the phenomena of Scripture. Embracing the humanity of the Bible is enormously helpful for understanding what's actually in the Bible—in terms of both its "untidiness" and its artistry.

56

The Father of Lights

The book of James deserves its reputation as one of the more practical, down-to-earth books in the New Testament. But while mining its riches for Christian living, we can easily overlook the powerful theological statements tucked away in this short letter. This one appears in the first chapter (Jas 1:17):

> Every good gift and every perfect gift is from above, coming down from the Father of lights with whom there is no variation or shadow due to change.

James' phrase "Father of lights" is unique in the Bible. Understanding the phrase is crucial to comprehending what he means by there being "no variation or shadow due to change" with God. "Father of lights" points to God's role as creator of the stars and other celestial objects. We see this idea in the creation account as well as in Psalms (Gen 1:14–18; Pss 136:7–9; 148:1–5). Similar phrases pointing to the same idea occur sporadically in other ancient Jewish literature, like the Dead Sea Scrolls.[1]

The celestial bodies mark seasons and the passage of time (Gen 1:14–18). They are associated with change. The word translated "change" (Greek *tropē*) in James 1:17 is a noun used elsewhere in Greek literature to describe the movement and positioning of stars, seasonal changes and their effect on the land, and the two annual solstices.[2] James' use of "change" with "shadow" suggests an eclipse. His point is profound. Although the lights—the celestial bodies—change and vary, their Father does not. He is unwavering.

But the phrase "Father of lights" conveys more than God's role as creator. His character and nature are fundamentally distinct from those of all other divine beings. Like those of other ancient cultures, Jewish writings convey the widespread belief that the stars were heavenly beings. This idea is found in the Old Testament, where the sons of God are metaphorically referred to as "the stars of God" (Job 38:7). James' description of God as the "Father of lights" then speaks of God as the creator of all heavenly beings—emphasizing that they are created and are therefore inferior. God alone is uncreated.

> *Although the lights—the celestial bodies—change and vary, their Father does not. He is unwavering.*

This idea also sheds light (pun intended) on 1 John 1:5, where John wrote that "God is light." His point was not that God is energy particles—which would mean that God is part of the creation, something John elsewhere explicitly denies (John 1:1-3). Rather, John uses the phrase metaphorically and qualifies it by saying that in God "there is no darkness at all." Only God is wholly true and good.

Our Father of lights stands alone as the one who created time and its markers. The celestial bodies move as he ordained at creation, while his nature remains constant.

The Author of change does not himself change. His character never fluctuates. The Father of lights created the spiritual beings who are his heavenly host (1 Kgs 22:19), but only he is consistently true and good. Their nature may fail. His will not.

57

What Do Demons Believe about God?

Like many other cinema fans, I count the romantic comedy *The Princess Bride* as one of my favorite movies of all time. It's filled with memorable characters and dialogue. For instance, the character Vizzini (who fancies himself a genius) is best remembered for repeatedly exclaiming, "Inconceivable!" He says it so often and in so many inappropriate contexts that it becomes silly—which is, of course, the intention. In one scene, Inigo Montoya points out the absurdity when he says to Vizzini, "You keep using that word; I do not think it means what you think it means."

I'm reminded of this line whenever I hear someone quote—or misquote—James 2:19: "You believe that God is one; you do well. Even the demons believe—and shudder!" The verse doesn't say what many readers presume it says.

Reading James Correctly

Over the years, I've heard this verse cited in an attempt to explain that the message of the gospel involves much more than just believing in God: "The demons believe in God, and that doesn't get them to heaven." It's true that simply believing there's a God won't get anyone to heaven. But James' point isn't that demons believe in God.

Look at the verse again. What the demons believe, according to James, is "that God is one." The demons believe in the existence of God, but James goes beyond that to tell us that the demons believe something specific about God—and that specific belief is what makes them shudder.

The Shema

The wording of James 2:19—"God is one"—is an echo of Deuteronomy 6:4: "Hear O Israel: The LORD our God, the LORD is one." This verse, considered the fundamental creed of believing Israelites, is called the Shema. That term is a transliteration of the command "Hear!"—which in Hebrew is the word *shemaʿ*.

James wrote his book to Jews who had come to believe in Jesus (Jas 1:1-3), so his readers would have picked up on the phrase and understood the reference. James is telling Jewish Christians that it's a good thing to believe that God is one. Their faith in Jesus as God doesn't require them to deny this fundamental point of biblical theology. But correct belief must be validated by righteous living.

James isn't arguing here that our works merit eternal life, as though God owes salvation to someone who has good works. God is never in the debt of any person at any time. Salvation cannot be earned (Eph 2:8-9). Rather, James wants to be able to discern the faith of his readers. Their works will show him (and others) that they believe—because one's belief in the truth is validated by the testimony of one's actions. We do not do good work to force God to give us our due, as though he owes us salvation. We work to show that we believe the gospel—his gracious offer of a salvation we could never earn.

What's So Scary about the *Shema*?

Demons, of course, may hold the correct belief that "God is one," but salvation was never offered to them. The crucial point of the Shema is that God offered redemption through the people of Israel, Abraham's descendants. In the Old Testament story, Israel was created through supernatural intervention after God dispersed the nations of the earth at the Tower of Babel (Gen 10; 11:1–9). Deuteronomy 32:8–9 describes what happened:

> When the Most High gave to the nations their inheritance, when he divided mankind, he fixed the borders of the peoples according to the number of the sons of God. But the LORD's portion is his people, Jacob his allotted heritage.[1]

After the judgment at the Tower of Babel, God called Abraham (Gen 12:1–3). The two events happened back to back. When God called Abraham and established his "portion"—the nation of Israel—he set aside all other nations. Those disinherited nations were allotted to other divine beings, the sons of God, who are elsewhere called the "host of heaven" (Deut 4:19; 17:3), gods (Hebrew *elohim*), and demons (Hebrew *shedim*) in Deuteronomy (4:19–20; 17:3; 29:24–26; 32:17).[2] We aren't told just when or how, but these sons of God set over the other nations became corrupt and abused their authority (Ps 82) by seducing the Israelites to worship them instead of the true God (Deut 29:24–26; 32:17).

What It All Means

The important theological point is that the people of those nations and the demon-gods to whom they were given were outside the plan of salvation. The rebellious sons of God, the demons (32:17), knew what the Shema meant. It reminded them that they were forever banished from the presence of the true God. It shouldn't surprise us that they trembled at the thought. For the Israelites, "The LORD our God is one" was a reminder that there was only one God who could provide salvation, and that God had chosen Israel out of the nations to be his own people. Only the Israelites had the truth about the Most High God: God had become incarnate in Christ. By embracing Jesus, James' audience was embracing the ultimate outcome of their ancient covenant faith.

> *The Shema reminded the rebellious sons of God, the demons, that they were forever banished from the presence of the true God.*

58

Jesus, the Morning Star out of Jacob

Chances are good that any talk about Jesus and a star you'll hear during the Christmas season will be about the events of Matthew 2:1–12, which tells of the magi following the celestial sign to the home of Joseph, Mary, and little Jesus. While that familiar story deserves the attention it gets, our fascination with it distracts from another star associated with the Messiah. In Numbers 24:17, we read the prophecy that "a star will go out from Jacob, and a scepter will rise from Israel" (LEB). You might think that this was the Old Testament prophecy Matthew had in mind when he wrote about the magi, but it wasn't. Matthew never quotes or alludes to this verse.

Numbers 24:17 was considered messianic in ancient Jewish thinking, but no one thought of a celestial sign when reading it. The star wasn't described as coming from the heavens; rather, it would "go out from Jacob" and "rise from Israel," and that means the star represents a person. In ancient times, star language was used to refer to divinity or royalty. Sometimes those conceptions merged, since kings were thought to be installed by the gods to rule or even to have divine parentage. For Israelites, star language pointed to the Messiah-King. Numbers 24:17 is therefore the backdrop for interpreting some odd passages in Revelation. Look at what the apostle John reports Jesus saying:

> And the one who conquers and who keeps my works until the end, I will give him authority over the nations, and "he will shepherd them with an iron rod; he will break them in pieces like jars made of clay," as I also have received from my Father, and I will give him the morning star. (Rev 2:25–28 LEB)

What does it mean to "give the morning star" to the one who conquers and remains faithful to Jesus? The answer lies in the parallel phrase earlier in the passage: To "give the morning star" means to "give authority over the nations" (v. 26). But precisely what that points to might still be a bit fuzzy. John clears it up in Revelation 22:16, where Jesus himself describes his messianic status using morning-star language:

> I am the root and the descendant of David, the bright morning star. (LEB)

In other words, Jesus is the divine messiah-king foretold in Numbers 24:17. The implication of this language and these passages is staggering. In Revelation 2:27, Jesus quotes Psalm 2:7–9, a psalm about his reign over the nations, and applies it to faithful believers. Jesus is and has the morning star. He is the messianic authority to rule the nations—and he intends to share that authority with his children. John repeats this thought in Revelation 3:21:

The one who conquers, I will grant to him to sit down with me on my throne, as I also have conquered and have sat down with my Father on his throne. (LEB)

The star of Bethlehem isn't the only star that makes Christmas wonderful. The one who is the morning star has decreed that believers' destiny involves not just an eternal home with God, but a shared rulership with our king on the new earth.

59

Relying on Our Preconceptions

Part of being a conscientious Bible student is ensuring we don't filter Scripture through our own assumptions and preconceived ideas about what it says. Our theology should come from the biblical text, not from our traditional readings of it.

Suspending our presuppositions is not as easy as it might seem. One of the more surprising examples of a misguided assumption involves the idea that the devil rebelled with one-third of God's angels in the primeval past, before the fall of humanity in Genesis 3. There is no passage in Scripture that records this event, yet many Christians believe it to be a point of biblical teaching. Only one passage in Scripture uses the term "third" in connection with language that could describe angels: Revelation 12:1–9:

> And a great sign appeared in heaven: a woman clothed with the sun. ... She was pregnant and was crying out in birth pains and the agony of giving birth. And another sign appeared in heaven: behold, a great red dragon, with seven heads and ten horns, and on his heads seven diadems. **His tail swept down a third of the stars of heaven and cast**

them to the earth. And the dragon stood before the woman who was about to give birth, so that when she bore her child he might devour it. She gave birth to a male child, one who is to rule all the nations with a rod of iron, but her child was caught up to God and to his throne, and the woman fled into the wilderness. ... Now war arose in heaven, Michael and his angels fighting against the dragon. And the dragon and his angels fought back, but he was defeated, and there was no longer any place for them in heaven. And the great dragon was thrown down, that ancient serpent, who is called the Devil and Satan, the deceiver of the whole world—**he was thrown down to the earth, and his angels were thrown down with him.**

The passage clearly identifies the dragon as the devil (12:9), and most scholars would identify the stars that were "cast down" (*ballō*; 12:4) to the earth with the dragon's angels, who ultimately were "thrown down" (*ballō*; 12:9). But this war in heaven is not connected explicitly with creation, a time before creation, or the fall of humanity; it's clearly associated with the birth of the Messiah (12:5), since the writer uses messianic wording for the child's destiny (Ps 2:9; Zech 9:10). In addition, the passage says nothing about when the devil turned from God.

Also, there are ambiguities in the passage. The actual mention of a war comes only in Rev 12:7, which describes the dragon (the devil) and his angels

There is no passage in Scripture that reports a third of God's angels rebelled with Satan.

fighting against Michael and his angelic warriors. That raises the possibility that the third of the angels ("stars" in 12:4) are not the devil's agents, but instead are godly angels defeated by the devil and other angels loyal to him. It is an assumption that the battle scene in 12:7–9 is expanding on the event in 12:4. They could be two separate events in the same overarching conflict.

In any case, the timing of the heavenly war is not what many Bible students presume. The apocalyptic nature of this text means we cannot be certain about any interpretation. As we study the Bible, it's all too easy to let well worn (and flawed) assumptions fill in the gaps in our understanding, especially when it comes to difficult passages. If we seek to be faithful to God's word, we need to be careful that we aren't reading it with preconceived interpretations in mind.

60

Jesus, Our Warrior

Most Bible students rightly associate the subject of holy war with the Old Testament. In books like Numbers, Deuteronomy, Joshua, and Judges, the Israelites often engage in combat against the hostile occupants of the promised land in the name of—and with aid from—Yahweh.

Holy war and its themes are so prevalent that many Christians cannot conceive how the God of the Old Testament is consistent with the divine father figure of the New Testament and especially with God incarnate in Jesus Christ. However, these portrayals of God are not contradictions. In fact, Jesus is cast as the divine warrior in the New Testament. Paul's letter to the Ephesians provides part of this portrait.

Old Testament Holy War Ideology

The Old Testament outlines rules and contexts for holy war (e.g., Deut 7, 20) that were put into practice during Israel's conflicts. Before the Israelites went to war, they were to consult God and discern his will (1 Sam 23:1–6). When God gave them the victory, they were to to destroy their enemy's military power and "put all its males to the sword" (Deut 20:13). In holy war, Yahweh was Israel's divine warrior—

the one who led the Israelites into battle and gave them victory (Exod 15; Josh 5:13–15; 6:1–2, 27).

Eventually God chose the man after his own heart, David, to be king over his people (1 Sam 16). God made a covenant with David legitimizing his dynastic line for the rest of Israel's history. Only David's descendants would have the right of kingship over Yahweh's people (2 Sam 7). Only a son of David would be God's approved protector of his people against the nations and their gods, sinister powers of darkness (Deut 32:8–9 ESV).[1]

The Warrior Messiah's Victory

The messianic Son of David is the ultimate King of Israel. The divine messiah, Jesus, is portrayed in the New Testament as a warrior-king using themes of Old Testament holy warfare. Perhaps the most familiar depiction of Jesus as divine warrior occurs in the book of Revelation. The end times and its apocalyptic struggle against the nations and the powers of darkness are a logical corollary to Old Testament holy war. The return of

> *The divine messiah, Jesus, is portrayed in the New Testament as a warrior-king using themes of Old Testament holy warfare.*

Jesus at the climax of the eschatological Day of the Lord is a familiar warfare scene, with Jesus at the head of God's army (Rev 19:11–21).

Outside Revelation, New Testament passages use the divine-warrior theme differently, in non-eschatological ways. In Ephesians 4:8–12, for instance, Paul frames Jesus' death and resurrection and the coming of the Spirit, against the backdrop of Yahweh's conquest of Mount

Bashan (Ps 68:15–18). Bashan was long associated with the giant clan enemies (the Rephaim) defeated by Moses and Joshua in holy war. Bashan was also home to the cities Ashtaroth and Edrei (Deut 1:4; 3:1), places considered in Canaanite religion to be gateways to the underworld.[2] This context of divine conquest frames the descriptions of Jesus as an enthroned king, now victorious over his enemies:

> [God] raised him from the dead and seated him at his right hand in the heavenly places, far above all rule and authority and power and dominion, and above every name that is named, not only in this age but also in the one to come. (Eph 1:20–21)

The Warrior Messiah Empowers His Spiritual Warriors

Old Testament holy-war theology is the backdrop for what is perhaps the most well-known passage on spiritual warfare in the New Testament. In Ephesians 6:11–12, Paul tells believers:

> Put on the whole armor of God, that you may be able to stand against the schemes of the devil. For we do not wrestle against flesh and blood, but against the rulers, against the authorities, against the cosmic powers over this present darkness, against the spiritual forces of evil in the heavenly places.

The details of the armor that follow (6:13–20) should be read within the scope of the real message: The Spirit of Yahweh, the divine warrior of Israel, will fight for you.

In true holy-war ideology, the real power is not found in human participants, but in the power of Jesus, our divine warrior-king.

Abbreviations

ABD *Anchor Bible Dictionary*. Edited by D. N. Freedman. 6 vols. 1992.

BDAG W. Bauer, F. W. Danker, W. F. Arndt, and F. W. Gingrich. *A Greek-English Lexicon of the New Testament and Other Early Christian Literature*. 3rd ed. 2000.

DDD *Dictionary of Deities and Demons in the Bible*. Edited by K. van der Toorn, B. Becking, and P. W. van der Horst. 2nd rev. ed. 1999.

DPL *Dictionary of Paul and His Letters*. Edited by G. F. Hawthorne and R. P. Martin. 1993.

FSB *Faithlife Study Bible*. Edited by J. D. Barry. Electronic ed. 2016.

HALOT *The Hebrew and Aramaic Lexicon of the Old Testament*. L. Koehler, W. Baumgartner, and J. J. Stamm. Electronic ed. 1994–2000.

LBD *Lexham Bible Dictionary*. Edited by J. D. Barry. 2016.

LEH J. Lust, E. Eynikel, and K. Hauspie. *A Greek-English Lexicon of the Septuagint*. Rev. ed. 2003.

LES *The Lexham English Septuagint*. Edited by Rick Brannan, Ken M. Penner, Israel Loken, Michael Aubrey, and Isaiah Hoogendyk. 2012.

LSJ H. G. Liddell, R. Scott, and H. S. Jones. *A Greek-English Lexicon*. 9th ed. with rev. supp. 1996.

TLOT *Theological Lexicon of the Old Testament*. Edited by E. Jenni and C. Westermann. 3 vols. 1997.

Bibliography

Annus, Amar. "On the Origin of Watchers: A Comparative Study of the Antediluvian Wisdom in Mesopotamian and Jewish Traditions." *Journal for the Study of the Pseudepigrapha* 19 (2010): 277–320.

Barry, John D., ed. *Faithlife Study Bible*. Bellingham, WA: Lexham Press, 2016.

———. *Lexham Bible Dictionary*. Bellingham, WA: Lexham Press, 2016.

Batto, Bernard F. "The Reed Sea: *Requiescat in Pace*." *Journal of Biblical Literature* 102 (1983): 27–35.

Bauer, Walter, Frederick W. Danker, William F. Arndt, and F. Wilbur Gingrich. *A Greek-English Lexicon of the New Testament and Other Early Christian Literature*. 3rd ed. Chicago: University of Chicago Press, 2000.

Brannan, Rick, trans. *The Apostolic Fathers in English*. Bellingham, WA: Lexham Press, 2012.

Brannan, Rick, Ken M. Penner, Israel Loken, Michael Aubrey, and Isaiah Hoogendyk, eds. *The Lexham English Septuagint*. Bellingham, WA: Lexham Press, 2012.

Darwin, Charles. *On the Origin of Species by Means of Natural Selection, or the Preservation of Favoured Races in the Struggle for Life*. London: John Murray, Albemarle Street, 1859.

Day, John. *From Creation to Babel: Studies in Genesis 1–11*. London: Bloomsbury Academic, 2013.

Dever, William G. *Did God Have a Wife? Archaeology and Folk Religion in Ancient Israel*. Grand Rapids: Eerdmans, 2008.

Engels, Friedrich. "Progress of Social Reform on the Continent." *The New Moral World*. November 4, 1843.

Feldman, Louis H., trans. *Judean Antiquities 1–4*. Vol. 3 of *Flavius Josephus: Translation and Commentary*, edited by Steve Mason. Leiden: Brill, 2000.

Flesher, Paul V. M., and Bruce Chilton. *The Targums: A Critical Introduction*. Waco, TX: Baylor University Press, 2011.

Freedman, David Noel, ed. *Anchor Bible Dictionary*. 6 vols. New York: Doubleday, 1992.

Harrison, R. K. *Introduction to the Old Testament*. Grand Rapids: Eerdmans, 1969.

Hawthorne, Gerald F., and Ralph P. Martin, eds. *Dictionary of Paul and His Letters*. Downers Grove, IL: InterVarsity Press, 1993.

Heiser, Michael S. *The Unseen Realm: Recovering the Supernatural Worldview of the Bible*. Bellingham, WA: Lexham Press, 2015.

———. *Supernatural: What the Bible Teaches about the Unseen World— And Why It Matters*. Bellingham, WA: Lexham Press, 2015.

———. *I Dare You Not to Bore Me with the Bible*. Bellingham, WA: Lexham Press, 2014.

Heiser, Michael S., H. H. Hardy, and Charles Otte. *Hebrew and Canaanite Inscriptions with English Translation*. Bellingham, WA: Lexham Press, 2008.

Hess, Richard S. *Israelite Religions: An Archaeological and Biblical Survey*. Grand Rapids: Baker Academic, 2007.

Horner, Jack, and James Gorman, *How to Build a Dinosaur: Extinction Doesn't Have to be Forever*. New York: Dutton, 2009.

Jenni, Ernst, and Claus Westermann, eds. *Theological Lexicon of the Old Testament*. Translated by Mark E. Biddle. Peabody, MA: Hendrickson Publishers, 1997.

Joüon, Paul, and Takamitsu Muraoka. *A Grammar of Biblical Hebrew*. rev. Eng. ed. Roma: Pontificio Istituto Biblico, 2006.

Keating, Karl. *The New Geocentrists*. El Cajon, CA: Rasselas House, 2015.

Keil, Carl F., and Franz Delitzsch. *Commentary on the Old Testament*. 10 vols. Peabody, MA: Hendrickson, 1996.

Kidd, Colin. *The Forging of Races: Race and Scripture in the Protestant Atlantic World, 1600–2000*. Cambridge: Cambridge University Press, 2006.

Kilmer, Anne Draffkorn. "The Mesopotamian Counterparts of the Biblical Nepilim." Pages 39–44 in *Perspectives on Language and Text: Essays and Poems in Honor of Francis I. Andersen's Sixtieth Birthday July 28, 1985*, eds. E. W. Conrad and E. G. Newing. Winona Lake, IN: Eisenbrauns, 1987.

Kitchen, K. A. *On the Reliability of the Old Testament*. Grand Rapids: Eerdmans, 2006.

Koehler, Ludwig, Walter Baumgartner, and Johann Jakob Stamm. *The Hebrew and Aramaic Lexicon of the Old Testament*. Translated and edited under the supervision of M. E. J. Richardson. Electronic ed. Leiden: Brill, 1994–2000.

Levenson, Jon D. "Poverty and the State in Biblical Thought." *Judaism* 25 (1976): 230–41.

Lichtheim, Miriam. *Ancient Egyptian Literature: Volume II: The New Kingdom*. Berkeley: University of California Press, 1976.

Liddell, H. G., R. Scott, and H. S. Jones. *A Greek-English Lexicon*. 9th ed. with rev. supp. Oxford: Clarendon, 1996.

Livingstone, David N. *Adam's Ancestors: Race, Religion, and the Politics of Human Origins*. Baltimore: Johns Hopkins University Press, 2008.

Lust, Johan, Erik Eynikel, and Katrin Hauspie, eds. *A Greek-English Lexicon of the Septuagint*. Rev. ed. Stuttgart: Deutsche Bibelgesellschaft, 2003.

Maier, Aren M. "A New Interpretation of the Term 'opalim in the Light of Recent Archaeological Finds in Philistia." *Journal for the Study of the Old Testament* 32 (2007): 23–40.

McDonald, Lee Martin. *The Biblical Canon: Its Origin, Transmission, and Authority*. Grand Rapids: Hendrickson, 2011.

McNamara, Martin. *Targum Neofiti 1: Genesis*. Vol. 1A of *The Aramaic Bible*, edited by Kevin Cathcart, Michael Maher, and Martin McNamara. Collegeville, MN: Liturgical Press, 1992.

Metzger, Bruce M. *A Textual Commentary on the Greek New Testament*. 2nd ed. New York: United Bible Societies, 1994.

Myers, Eric. "Secondary Burials in Palestine." *Biblical Archaeologist* 33.2 (1970): 2–29

Snaith, Norman H. "יַם־סוּף: The Sea of Reeds: The Red Sea." *Vetus Testamentum* 15 (1965): 395–98.

Toorn, Karel van der, Bob Becking, and Pieter W. van der Horst, eds. *Dictionary of Deities and Demons in the Bible*. 2nd ed. Leiden: Brill, 1999.

Waltke, Bruce K. *The Book of Proverbs, Chapters 15–31*. Grand Rapids: Eerdmans, 2005.

Walton, John H. "Exodus, Date Of." Pages 258–72 in *Dictionary of the Old Testament: Pentateuch*. Edited by T. Desmond Alexander and David W. Baker. Downers Grove, IL: InterVarsity Press, 2003.

Wildberger, Hans. *Isaiah 28–39: A Continental Commentary*. Translated by Thomas H. Trapp. Minneapolis, MN: Fortress Press, 2002.

Wood, Bryant G. "Did the Israelites Conquer Jericho? A New Look at the Archaeological Evidence." *Biblical Archaeology Review* 16.2 (1990): 44–59.

Wyatt, Nicolas. "Cain's Wife." *Folklore* 97 (1986): 88–95.

Notes

INTRODUCTION
1. Michael S. Heiser, *I Dare You Not to Bore Me with the Bible* (Bellingham, WA: Lexham Press, 2014), x.
2. Many of the articles in this collection originally appeared in *Bible Study Magazine*; others were drawn from a series I did on the *Logos Academic Blog* (https://academic.logos.com/). Several of the longer articles have not been published previously.

CHAPTER 1: SERIOUS BIBLE STUDY ISN'T FOR SISSIES
1. BDAG stands for "Bauer, Danker, Arndt, Gingrich" and refers to the standard scholarly lexicon of New Testament Greek prepared by Walter Bauer, Frederick W. Danker, William F. Arndt, and F. Wilbur Gingrich, *A Greek-English Lexicon of the New Testament and Other Early Christian Literature*, 3rd ed. (Chicago: University of Chicago Press, 2000).

CHAPTER 2: GETTING SERIOUS—AND BEING HONEST—
ABOUT INTERPRETING THE BIBLE IN CONTEXT
1. Tertullian lived around AD 160–225. Irenaeus lived around AD 130–200. Augustine lived around AD 354–430.
2. Late Antiquity is the historical period from around AD 250–750 in the ancient Mediterranean and the ancient Near East. The Middle Ages are the period of European history from roughly the fall of Rome in the 5th century AD to the beginning of the Renaissance in the 15th century AD. The Protestant Reformation took place in western Europe in the 16th century AD. The Puritans were a group of English Protestants, mainly associated with the 16th–17th centuries AD.

CHAPTER 3: SINCERITY AND THE SUPERNATURAL

1. See Michael S. Heiser, *The Unseen Realm: Recovering the Supernatural Worldview of the Bible* (Bellingham, WA: Lexham Press, 2015), 32–36.
2. Heiser, *Unseen Realm*, 32.

CHAPTER 4: LET THE BIBLE BE WHAT IT IS

1. For example, the Logos Mobile Education course collection "Learn to Use Biblical Greek and Hebrew with Logos 6."
2. Michael S. Heiser, *Supernatural: What the Bible Teaches about the Unseen World—And Why It Matters* (Bellingham, WA: Lexham Press, 2015).
3. Michael S. Heiser, "The Old Testament and the Ancient Near Eastern Worldview," *FSB*.

CHAPTER 5: BAD BIBLE INTERPRETATION
REALLY CAN HURT PEOPLE

1. A good deal of scholarly work has been done in recent years explaining how flawed Bible interpretation led to theories of race and racial superiority. See, for example, David N. Livingstone, *Adam's Ancestors: Race, Religion, and the Politics of Human Origins* (Baltimore: Johns Hopkins University Press, 2008); Colin Kidd, *The Forging of Races: Race and Scripture in the Protestant Atlantic World, 1600-2000* (Cambridge: Cambridge University Press, 2006).
2. Charles Darwin, *On the Origin of Species by Means of Natural Selection, or the Preservation of Favoured Races in the Struggle for Life* (London: John Murray, Albemarle Street, 1859).

CHAPTER 6: UNYIELDING LITERALISM:
YOU REAP WHAT YOU SOW

1. See, for example, Karl Keating, *The New Geocentrists* (El Cajon, CA: Rasselas House, 2015).
2. For a description of Old Testament cosmology, see my article "The Old Testament and the Ancient Near Eastern Worldview," *FSB*.

CHAPTER 9: MARXISM AND BIBLICAL
THEOLOGY AREN'T SYNONYMS

1. I've expanded on this in detail in a twelve part series on poverty and biblical theology on my blog, *The Naked Bible* (http://drmsh.com/category/biblical-theology-doctrine/social-justice/).

2. Jon D. Levenson, "Poverty and the State in Biblical Thought," *Judaism* 25 (1976): 230–41.
3. Levenson, "Poverty," 235.
4. Friedrich Engels, "Progress of Social Reform on the Continent," *The New Moral World*, November 4, 1843.

CHAPTER 10: HOW TO (MIS)INTERPRET PROPHECY

1. See chap. 6, "Unyielding Literalism: You Reap What You Sow."
2. Reflects the Hebrew word *'adam*.
3. The Hebrew term is *'edom*. The word for mankind and the name Edom are spelled with the same Hebrew consonants, *'dm*. The vowels were not explicitly marked in Hebrew texts of the first century AD. Vowel markings as we know them in biblical Hebrew texts today came into use with the Masoretes (ca. AD 600–1000).

CHAPTER 11: DID YAHWEH FATHER CAIN?

1. Literally, "I have gotten [*qanithi*] a man [*ish*] with YHWH [*eth-YHWH*]."
2. For example, N. Wyatt, "Cain's Wife," *Folklore* 97:1 (1986): 88–95 (esp. 88).

CHAPTER 12: ALL YOUR GENESIS COMMENTARIES ARE 8-TRACK TAPES

1. See Heiser, *Unseen Realm*, 92–108 for a detailed look at the interpretive options for Gen 6:1–4 and the connection between the sons of God and the Nephilim.
2. Amar Annus, "On the Origin of Watchers: A Comparative Study of the Antediluvian Wisdom in Mesopotamian and Jewish Traditions," *Journal for the Study of the Pseudepigrapha* 19 (2010): 277–320.
3. Such as: J. C. Greenfield, "Apkallu," *DDD* 72–74; Anne Draffkorn Kilmer, "The Mesopotamian Counterparts of the Biblical Nepilim," *Perspectives on Language and Text: Essays and Poems in Honor of Francis I. Andersen's Sixtieth Birthday July 28, 1985*, eds. E. W. Conrad and E. G. Newing (Winona Lake, IN: Eisenbrauns, 1987): 39–44.

CHAPTER 13: WHAT'S IN A NAME?

1. The divine name should *not* be pronounced "Jehovah" (or "Yehovah" or "Yahovah"). "Jehovah" is a German spelling. In German, the letter "j" is pronounced like the English "y." The pronunciation and spelling of Jehovah arose in the Middle Ages as a misreading

of Hebrew scribal practices. The scribes refused to pronounce the divine name out of reverence. When they had to write it, they used the four consonants (*yhwh*) but swapped in the vowels from the word *adonay* ("lord") to indicate that *adonay* should be said aloud, not any variation using the consonants *yhwh*. The resulting combination of *yahovah* or *yehovah* is an artificial word—a misunderstanding that resulted from combining consonants and vowels that were not meant to be read together.

2. The Hebrew letters *waw* ("w") and *yod* ("y") came to be interchangeable in the spellings of some words.
3. See Ernst Jenni, "Yahweh," *TLOT* 522.
4. In very ancient Hebrew and Aramaic, the *yi-* prefix derived from the *ya-* prefix. See Paul Joüon and Takamitsu Muraoka, *A Grammar of Biblical Hebrew*, rev. Eng. ed. (Roma: Pontificio Istituto Biblico, 2006), 118 [§41e]. It is possible that this is what has happened with the divine name.

CHAPTER 14: LOST AT SEA

1. While Exod 14 only refers to the body of water blocking Israel's path as the "sea" (*yam*), many other passages referring to the event refer to the sea as the *yam suph* (e.g., Exod 13:18; 15:4; Deut 11:4; Josh 2:10; 4:23; 24:6; Neh 9:9; Pss 106:9; 136:15).
2. Num 33:8–10. Emphasis added.
3. On this interpretation, see Norman H. Snaith. "יַם־סוּף: The Sea of Reeds: The Red Sea." *Vetus Testamentum* 15 (1965): 395–98; and Bernard F. Batto, "The Reed Sea: *Requiescat in Pace*," *Journal of Biblical Literature* 102 (1983): 27–35.

CHAPTER 16: THE ANGEL OF YAHWEH
IN THE OLD TESTAMENT

1. In this quotation of Judg 6:12–17, 21–23, bold text has been added for emphasis, the referent of several pronouns has been noted explicitly, and the text has been formatted as dialogue with a new paragraph marking a change in speaker. The translation is the LEB.
2. Metzger observes that "Jesus" is the "best attested reading among Greek and versional witnesses" (Bruce M. Metzger, *A Textual Commentary on the Greek New Testament*, 2nd ed. [New York: United Bible Societies, 1994], 657). See also Heiser, *Unseen Realm*, 270n9.

CHAPTER 18: WHERE THE WILD (DEMONIC) THINGS ARE

1. See the relevant entries in the *Dictionary of Deities and Demons in the Bible (DDD)*.

2. Many commentators treat them as such (e.g., C. F. Keil and F. Delitzsch, *Commentary on the Old Testament*, 10 vols. [Peabody, MA: Hendrickson, 1996], 7:198).

3. LSJ, s.v. "ὀνοκενταύρα."

4. LEH, s.v. "ὀνοκένταυρος."

5. Most commentators who take the animals in verse 13 as simply wild animals allow that the creatures named in verse 14 may represent demonic beings. Hans Wildberger notes that the imagery involves sinister animals and demonic creatures, but the passage blurs the line between the two (*Isaiah 28-39: A Continental Commentary* [Minneapolis, MN: Fortress Press, 2002], 335).

6. See M. Hutter, "Lilith," *DDD* 520-21.

CHAPTER 20: THE ONGOING BATTLE OF JERICHO

1. For a thorough overview of the debate over the date of the exodus, see John H. Walton, "Exodus, Date of" in *Dictionary of the Old Testament: Pentateuch*, ed. T. Desmond Alexander and David W. Baker (Downers Grove, IL: InterVarsity Press, 2016), 258-72.

2. For a history of the archaeological debate in the early to mid-twentieth century, see R. K. Harrison, *Introduction to the Old Testament* (Grand Rapids: Eerdmans, 1969), 174-77.

3. For a discussion of the archaeological data related to the conquest of Canaan, see T. Michael Kennedy, "Canaan, Conquest of," *LBD*.

4. See Bryant G. Wood, "Did the Israelites Conquer Jericho? A New Look at the Archaeological Evidence," *Biblical Archaeology Review* 16.2 (1990): 44-59.

5. E.g., K. A. Kitchen, "Exodus, The," *ABD* 2:702-703; compare K. A. Kitchen, *On the Reliability of the Old Testament* (Grand Rapids: Eerdmans, 2006), 307-310.

CHAPTER 21: SCRIPTURE'S SACRED TREES

1. The terms for terebinth and oak are interchangeable (see Irene Jacob and Walter Jacob, "Flora," *ABD*, 2:806).

2. Heiser, *Dare You*, 173-75.

CHAPTER 22: BOAZ—THE LAWBREAKER?

1. Later rabbinic teaching took note of Ruth's conversion, adding that Deuteronomy 23:3 refers only to *men* from Ammon and Moab since the Hebrew word forms are masculine (see Sifre 249; m. Yevamot 8:3).

CHAPTER 23: OF MICE AND MANHOOD

1. For example, the LEB and the ESV both translate *ophalim* as "tumors."
2. The *Qere* word subsequently found its way into the running text of some Masoretic Bibles in 1 Sam 6:11, 17. The word *ophalim* occurs six times in the Old Testament, only once outside the context of the Philistine episode of 1 Sam 5-6. The exception is Deut 28:27 where the term is accompanied by descriptions of "scabs and itch," making a meaning of "tumors" likely. But no such qualifiers appear in the Philistine story.
3. The term became a proper name (Ophel) for the southeast ridge of ancient Jerusalem (2 Chr 27:3; Neh 3:26-27). Some scholars think this *ophel* is a homograph to that found in 1 Sam 5-6 (that is, a different word spelled exactly the same way).
4. Aren M. Maier, "A New Interpretation of the Term *'opalim* in the Light of Recent Archaeological Finds in Philistia," *Journal for the Study of the Old Testament* 32 (2007): 23-40.

CHAPTER 24: SAMUEL'S GHOST AND SAUL'S JUDGMENT

1. See J. Tropper, "Spirit of the Dead," *DDD* 806-809.

CHAPTER 26: DEFEATING ANCIENT FOES

1. See Heiser, "Rephaim," *LBD*.
2. The parallel in 1 Chr 20:6-8 spells *ha-raphah* with a different final letter (*ha-rapha'*) demonstrating that the two spellings are interchangeable. The latter spelling is used in the Hebrew for *rephaim*.

CHAPTER 27: YAHWEH AND HIS ASHERAH

1. The Hebrew/Canaanite inscriptions with this phrase come from Kuntillet Ajrud and Khirbet El-Qom. Transcriptions are available in Michael S. Heiser, H. H. Hardy, and Charles Otte, *Hebrew and Canaanite Inscriptions* (Bellingham, WA: Lexham Press, 2008). See Khirbet El-Qom 3 and Kuntillet Ajrud 14, 18, 19.1, 20.
2. Kuntillet Ajrud 18, line 2 (see Heiser, Hardy, and Otte, *Hebrew and Canaanite Inscriptions*).

3. For a detailed overview of the interpretation of these inscriptions, see Richard S. Hess, *Israelite Religions: An Archaeological and Biblical Survey* (Grand Rapids: Baker Academic, 2007), 283–90.
4. See Jeremiah K. Garrett with Douglas Mangum, "Goddess," *LBD*.
5. Ashtart is the goddess' Phoenician name. In Ugaritic, her name is spelled Athtartu. The Greek version is Astarte. In the Old Testament, her name often appears as "Ashtoreth" (e.g., 1 Kgs 11:5; see Peter B. Boeckel, "Ashtoreth," *LBD*).
6. See Eric Tully, "Asherah," *LBD*.
7. Hess, *Israelite Religions*, 283.
8. See chapter 21, "Scripture's Sacred Trees."
9. The Hebrew word for wisdom, *hokhmah*, is grammatically feminine.
10. Hess, *Israelite Religions*, 287–88.
11. William Dever argues that the inscriptions should be understood as evidence that some in ancient Israel believed Yahweh had a consort (*Did God Have a Wife? Archaeology and Folk Religion in Ancient Israel* [Grand Rapids: Eerdmans, 2008], 162–67).

CHAPTER 28: ANGELS AREN'T PERFECT
1. See 2 Pet 2:4–5; Jude 6.
2. Heiser, *Unseen Realm*, 92–123.

CHAPTER 30: JURASSIC BIBLE?
1. Jack Horner and James Gorman, *How to Build a Dinosaur: Extinction Doesn't Have to be Forever* (New York: Dutton, 2009). Horner was also the technical advisor for all the Jurassic Park films.
2. Douglas Mangum with Matthew James Hamilton, "Leviathan," *LBD*.
3. Mangum with Hamilton, "Leviathan," *LBD*.
4. See Trent C. Butler and Douglas Mangum, "Dragon and Sea," *LBD*; Douglas Mangum, "Rahab the Sea Monster," *LBD*.
5. Note that Psalm 74:12–17 uses combat creation imagery to also describe God's victory in the wilderness such as with the parting of the Red Sea and the conquest of Pharaoh.

CHAPTER 31: PROVERBS: THE WISDOM OF EGYPT?
1. Translation of *Amenemope* from Miriam Lichtheim, *Ancient Egyptian Literature: Volume II: The New Kingdom* (Berkeley: University of California Press, 1976), 146–62.

CHAPTER 32: HEAP BURNING COALS ON THEIR HEADS

1. See Bruce K. Waltke, *The Book of Proverbs: Chapters 15–31* (Grand Rapids: Eerdmans, 2005), 331.

CHAPTER 33: DENIAL OF THE AFTERLIFE

1. Others include Ecc 2:16; 3:19; 9:2–3.
2. See my article on "Old Testament Theology of the Afterlife," *FSB*.
3. The most common expressions are "gathered to his people" and "slept with his fathers"; the same idea is expressed a few times as being "gathered to their/your fathers" (Judg 2:10; 2 Kgs 22:20; 2 Chr 34:28).
4. For an excellent study on this, see Eric Myers, "Secondary Burials in Palestine," *Biblical Archaeologist* 33.2 (1970): 2–29 (esp. 15–17).

CHAPTER 34: SOLOMON'S BRIDE OR JESUS' BRIDE?

1. See Lee Martin McDonald, *The Biblical Canon: Its Origin, Transmission, and Authority* (Grand Rapids: Hendrickson, 2011), 111–13.
2. Christopher M. Jones, "Song of Songs, Book of, Critical Issues," *LBD*.
3. McDonald, *Canon*, 112–13.

CHAPTER 35: GOG OF THE SUPERNATURAL NORTH

1. See J. Lust, "Gog," *DDD* 373–75.

CHAPTER 36: FILTERING GOD

1. *HALOT*, s. v. "שׁוּר."

CHAPTER 38: ZECHARIAH'S DIVINE MESSIAH

1. See chap. 16, "The Angel of Yahweh in the Old Testament."
2. See chap. 36, "Filtering God."
3. See my article on "The Name Theology of the Old Testament," *FSB*.
4. Heiser, *Unseen Realm*, 270.

CHAPTER 40: DEMONS, SWINE, AND COSMIC GEOGRAPHY

1. Heiser, *Dare You*, 139–41.
2. Heiser, *Dare You*, 67–69.

CHAPTER 41: STRANGE AND POWERFUL SIGNS

1. Josephus, *Antiquities* 3.123; 3.180–181; see Louis H. Feldman, trans., *Judean Antiquities 1–4*, vol. 3, *Flavius Josephus: Translation and Commentary*, ed. Steve Mason (Leiden: Brill, 2000), 280n475.

2. Given the supernatural power of God, there is no need to deny the historicity of what Matthew describes. And, if we are to avoid inconsistency, such a decision would require rejecting the other elements of Matthew's post-resurrection description. Also, the phrase "after his resurrection" (Matt 27:53) gives priority to Jesus as the "firstfruits" of the resurrection (1 Cor 15:20, 23); it does not specify a time sequence (as though the dead were raised in their tombs when Jesus died but had to wait until his resurrection before they could emerge).

CHAPTER 42: IS EXORCISM FOR EVERYONE?

1. Katie Jagel, "Poll Results: Exorcism," YouGov, September 17, 2013, https://today.yougov.com/news/2013/09/17/poll-results-exorcism/.
2. See chap. 40, "Demons, Swine, and Cosmic Geography."
3. See, for example, the Testament of Joseph 6:1–8. The Testament of Joseph may date from 2nd century BC to 2nd century AD or later. There is debate whether the Testament was originally a Jewish or a Christian composition since the text as known has significant Christian interpolations (see Janghoon Park, "Testaments of the Twelve Patriarchs," *LBD*).

CHAPTER 43: THE WORD WAS GOD

1. On the targumic background of John's *logos* imagery, see Paul V. M. Flesher and Bruce Chilton, *The Targums: A Critical Introduction* (Waco, TX: Baylor University Press, 2011), 423–36.
2. There are three main Targums of the Pentateuch: Onqelos, Neofiti, and Pseudo-Jonathan. Targum Jonathan to the Prophets covers the Former Prophets and the Latter Prophets. Of these, Onqelos and Jonathan appear to have been the most important in rabbinic Judaism (Flesher and Chilton, *Targums*, 9).
3. The Targum translations in this article are my own.
4. Martin McNamara, *Targum Neofiti 1: Genesis*, vol. 1A of *The Aramaic Bible*, ed. Kevin Cathcart, Michael Maher, and Martin McNamara (Collegeville, MN: Liturgical Press, 1992), 37–38.

CHAPTER 44: THE TABLE OF NATIONS AND ACTS 2

1. The "Table of Nations" refers to the genealogical list in Gen 10. The list represents the known world from the time in which it was written by presenting the people groups of the ancient Near East and ancient Mediterranean according to the name of their

eponymous ancestor, that is, the person from whom the people took their name (see Michael S. Heiser, "Understanding the Table of Nations," *FSB*).

2. My translation.

3. The reading "sons of God" is also supported by the Septuagint, the Greek translation of the Old Testament that also reflects a textual tradition much older than the traditional Hebrew text.

CHAPTER 45: PAUL'S MISSIONARY GOALS

1. See chap. 43, "The Table of Nations and Acts 2."

2. While there is some debate over the location of Tarshish, John Day does an excellent job of demonstrating that Tarshish is located in Spain and not an Aegean location (see "Where was Tarshish [Gen 10:4]?" in *From Creation to Babel: Studies in Genesis 1–11* [London: Bloomsbury Academic, 2013], 154–165).

3. For more on Paul's desire to reach Spain, see Heiser, *Unseen Realm*, 302–306.

4. Rick Brannan, trans., *The Apostolic Fathers in English* (Bellingham, WA: Lexham Press, 2012), I Clement 5.5–7.

CHAPTER 46: DIVINE MISDIRECTION

1. Following the Dead Sea Scrolls; see ESV.

2. Theodotion's text of the Septuagint consistently reads *archōn* and *archontōn*. Other Septuagint manuscripts use other terms on occasion.

CHAPTER 48: NEW TESTAMENT LANGUAGE OF SPIRITUAL ADOPTION AND SONSHIP

1. Heiser, *Unseen Realm*, 110–15.

2. The following New Testament passages are representative of the language of sonship, adoption, and glorification as described here: Luke 20:34–36; John 1:11; Rom 8:15–23, 9:6–8; Eph 1:4–5, 2:19–22; Col 1:11–13; Heb 2:5–13; 1 John 3:1; 2 Pet 1:2–4.

CHAPTER 49: THE LORD, WHO IS THE SPIRIT

1. See my article on "Bashan and the Gates of Hell," *FSB*.

2. See also Rom 8:9–10; Phil 1:19; Gal 4:4–6; 1 Pet 1:10–11.

CHAPTER 51: WATCH YOUR LANGUAGE!

1. LSJ, s.v. "σκύβαλον."

CHAPTER 52: NO LONGER SLAVES

1. See Daniel G. Reid, "Elements/Elemental Spirits of the World," *DPL* 229. My listing is based on Reid's, but I have broken the possibilities down differently.

CHAPTER 53: THE RELATIONSHIP OF
BAPTISM AND CIRCUMCISION

1. Today the practice, often referred to as "female genital mutilation" (FGM), is strongly condemned by the international community. In December 2012, the United Nations passed a resolution calling for an end to the practice (http://www.un.org/apps/news/story. asp?NewsID=43839).
2. Heiser, *Dare You*, 17.

CHAPTER 54: DISARMING THE POWERS OF DARKNESS

1. Some translations (e.g., ESV) read "triumphing over them in him" at the end of v. 15. The Greek text allows for either translation, but the context points to the cross ("it").
2. See chap. 60, "Jesus Our Warrior." For a broader discussion of this topic, see *Unseen Realm*, chapters 14–15, 32–35.
3. Reading "sons of God" in Deut 32:8 with the Dead Sea Scrolls, as reflected in the ESV. See Heiser, *Dare You*, 67–69.

CHAPTER 55: INSPIRATION WAS A PROCESS, NOT AN EVENT

1. Compare Matthew and Mark's account of the temptation of Jesus: Matt 4:1–11; Mark 1:12–13.
2. Compare events that follow the calling of the Twelve between Matthew, Mark, and Luke (begin in Matt 10:1–4; Mark 3:13–19; Luke 6:12–15).

CHAPTER 56: THE FATHER OF LIGHTS

1. For example, "Father of light" (Testament of Abraham B 7:6), "Father of the universe / cosmos" (Philo, *De Specialibus Legibus* 1.96), and "prince of lights" (Damascus Document 5:18 and Manual of Discipline 3:20 from the Dead Sea Scrolls).
2. A solstice marks the time when the sun is at its greatest distance from the celestial equator. For *tropē* used in that sense, see Herodotus, *Hist.* 2.19; Thucydides, *Hist.* 7.16; and Wisdom of Solomon 7:18.

CHAPTER 57: WHAT DO DEMONS BELIEVE ABOUT GOD?

1. This is the reading of the ESV. In many English translations, Deuteronomy 32:8 reads "according to the sons of Israel." The ESV has the correct translation, since it uses the Dead Sea scroll manuscripts for translating this verse. Additionally, "sons of Israel" makes no sense in context, since Israel did not yet exist as a nation at the time of Babel—which is why "Israel" is not listed among the nations of the earth in Genesis 10.

2. On the various terms for divine beings, see Heiser, *Unseen Realm*, 30–34. On the allotment of the disinherited nations to other divine beings, see *Unseen Realm*, 110–15.

CHAPTER 60: JESUS, OUR WARRIOR

1. On the reality of the gods and the impact of this belief throughout the Old and New Testaments, see Heiser, *Unseen Realm*.

2. See Heiser, "Bashan and the Gates of Hell," *FSB*.

Scripture Index

Old Testament

Genesis

1	160–61
1:2	161
1:6	21
1:10	21
1:14–18	211
1:21	121
1:26	17, 186
2:9	93
3	30, 115, 221
3:8	167
3:15	186
4:1	49–50, 51
6:1–4	16, 53, 54–55, 115, 237n1
6:2	185
6:4	106, 185
10	169, 172–73, 216, 244n1, 246n1
10:2	139
10:4	244n2
11	172–73
11:1–9	32, 170, 179, 186, 206, 216
11:7	171–72
12:1–3	79, 170, 186, 216
12:6	111
12:6–7	92, 93
13:16	30
13:18	111
14:19	109
15:1	75, 93, 186
15:1–6	79
17:1–6	79
17:1–14	202
17:15–21	202
18	144
18:1	111
18:1–8	16
18:11–12	50
18:13–15	50
19:1–11	16
21:6–7	50
22:18	79
24:34–35	40
25	46
25:25	59
25:30	59
26:5	79
28:10–22	142, 144
31	65
31:11–13	71
31:19	65
31:34–45	65
32:22–32	16
32:24	141
32:28	141
32:30	141
35:1–7	142

35:4 92
36:1 46
48 71
48:15–16 .... 71, 142
49:29 134

Exodus
3:1–6 67–68
3:2 68
3:4 68
3:14 56–57
4:22–23 185
13:18 .... 238n1
14 .... 59, 238n1
15 225
15:2 57
15:3 109
15:4 .... 238n1
15:11 101
16:3 95
18 63
19:16 145
19:18 145
20–23 79
20:15 40
21 .... 63, 66
21:1–6 62–66
21:6 .... 63–64, 65
22:31 192
23 70
23:4 130
23:20–23 .... 68–69, 70, 74,
                          144, 148
23:21 69
23:23 70
23:31 60
28:30 9
32:1–24 81
33:20 .... 141, 142–43
34:13 110

Leviticus
4:20 80
4:26 80
4:31 80
4:35 80
5:10 80
5:13 80
5:16 80
5:18 80
6:7 80
10–11 79
11:7 158
13:1–14:57 32
15 32
15:19–24 9
16:17 95
17:7 81
23:34 45
25:39–43 96
25:46 96
25:54–55 96
26 79

Numbers
10:11 88
13:32–33 .... 16, 53
14:11 166–67
14:26–33 88
15:15 95
15:25–28 80
15:26 95
21:4 60
24:17 218–19
27:18–23 87
33:8–10 .... 60, 238n2

Deuteronomy
1:4 .... 188, 226
2:10–11 106
2:11 106

2:14...88
3:1.. 226
3:10–11 188
4:19.................................. 114, 216
4:19–20 ....169, 186, 206, 216
4:35..64
4:37..148
4:37–38 70
4:39 64
5–26 85
5:21..40
6:4..215
6:13..83
6:16..83
7... 224
7:3–5...186
7:7 203
7:35.. 202
8:3 83
10:16 .... 80, 202
11:4 ....238n1
12..64
12:4..70
12:11..70
12:21 70
14:1 185
14:23 70
15:2–3 96
15:12–18................................ 63
16:2..70
16:6 70
16:11..70
17:2–3 206
17:3..216
17:14–17................................103
18:9–14................................. 102
18:11..133
20.. 224
20:13...................................... 224
21:10–14 96

21:16 40
23:3.....................94, 95, 240n1
23:12–14 196
23:17–18 192
23:19–20 96
24:14.. 41
25:5–10 94
27 85
27:3.. 85
27:9–14 85
28:27 ....240n2
29..85–86
29:24–26...................... 206, 216
29:29 .... 84–85, 86
30:6............................. 80, 202
31:7–8 87
32 .... 170, 172
32:8 ....172, 185, 245n3, 246n1
32:8–9 .... 115, 159, 162, 169–70,
179, 186, 206, 216, 225
32:17 .... 65, 101, 115, 179, 183,
206, 216

Joshua

2:6...89
2:10 ....238n1
2:11–12 96
3:15..89
4:9...89
4:23....................................238n1
5:10..89
5:13–15 .... 69, 70, 225
6.. 87
6:1–2 225
6:25 96
6:27 225
7:24 88
8:35 95
9:10 188
11:22 106

12:4–5 188
13:3 106
14:12 105
15:8 107
15:13–14 105
18:16 107
24 91
24:6 ....238n1
24:6–8 69
24:15 91
24:24–26 91
24:26 92

Judges

2:1–2 148
2:1–3 69
2:10 .... 242n3
2:13 109
3:7 110
3:11 90
3:31 90
4:4–5 93
6 72–73
6:12–17 .... 72–73, 238n1
6:21 73
6:21–23 ....73, 238n1
6:23 73
6:25–26 110
8:28 90
9:5–6 92
9:34–37 93
11:16 60
17–21 32
21:5 95
21:8 95

Ruth

1:3–5 94
1:4 94
1:6–19 94

1:16 96
4:9–10 94
4:10 94

1 Samuel

1:19–20 51
3:21 75
4:11–22 97
4:18 90
5–6 .... 97, 240n2, 240n3
5:1–2 97
5:3–5 97
5:6 97
6:4–18 98
6:5 98
6:11 ....240n2
6:17 .... 98, 240n2
14:49 103
14:50 104
16 225
17:4 106
18:27–28 103
19:13 65
19:16 65
23:1–6 224
25 104
25:1 101
25:1–2 104
25:3 104
25:39–43 103
25:43–44 104
25:44 103
28 100
28:3 101
28:3–7 100
28:3–20 16
28:7 101
28:8–11 100
28:13 ....65, 133
28:13–14 100

28:15 101
28:16–19 101
30:31 105

2 Samuel

2:2 104
2:10 90
2:11 105
3:12–16 104
5:4 90
5:5 105
5:13 103
5:18 107
5:22 107
7... 225
12:7–8 104
16:9 192
21 106
21:16–22 106
21:22 106
22 145
22:8 21
22:12–16 146
23:13 107

1 Kings

2:10 134
2:11 90
6:1 .... 87, 88, 90
8..70
9:26 60
11:5 ....109, 241n5
11:33 109
11:42 90
12:3 95
13:14 93
14:11 192
14:23 110
18:19 110
22:19 ....114, 213

22:19–23 117

2 Kings

18:4 110
21:3 ....110, 114
21:7 110
22–23 65
22:20 ....134, 242n3
23:4 110
24–25 187

1 Chronicles

11:15 ....81, 107
20:5 107
20:6–8 ....240n2

2 Chronicles

2:50–51 105
11:5–12 105
27:3...................................240n3
30:25 95
34:28 .... 242n3

Ezra

9–10 32
10 95
10:10–19 95
10:44 95

Nehemiah

3:26–27 ....240n3
9:6 101
9:9 ....238n1
13:23 95
13:23–27 95

Job

1:6 185
1:6–11 116
1:6–2:1 116

1:9–12 116
2:1 185
3:8 121
4:17–18 116–17
4:18 .... 113, 114
5:1 .... 113, 117
10:21 161
11:7–10 116
15:14–16 114
15:15 113
17:11–16 161
25 114
25:4–5 113
33:23 117–18
33:23–24 116
36:29–30 145
38:4–7 114
38:7 212
38:17 .... 161, 185
41:1 121

Psalms

2:7 185
2:7–9 219
2:9 222
16:3 114
18:7 161
18:11 145
18:15 161
20:1 70
20:7 70
22:12 205
34:9 114
41:12 133
68 ....188–89, 205
68:15 188
68:15–18 225–26
68:16 188
68:18 ....188, 189
73:23–24 133

73:26 133
74:12–14 123
74:12–17 .... 241n5
74:14 121
77:17–18 145
82 .... 115, 206, 216
82:1 .... 63, 65, 101, 116
82:1–4 159
82:5 161
82:6–8 159
89:5 ....113, 159
89:5–6 116
89:6 185
89:7 113
89:8–9 158
89:9–11 123
89:27 185
104:3 145
104:5 ....28, 161
104:26 121
106:9 ....238n1
136:2 101
136:7–9 211
136:15 ....238n1
139:13 50
148:1–5 211

Proverbs

1:7 ....124, 130
6:27–28 131
8:22–31 111
8:27–28 21
9:10 ....124, 130
10:4 40
13:4 40
14:31 41
15:33 128
19:14 40
22–23 124–28
22:17 124

22:17–18 125
22:20 125
22:22 125
22:24 125
22:28 126
23:10–11 126
23:1–3 .... 126, 127
23:4–5 127
24:17–18 130
25:21 130
25:21–22 129
25:22 .... 129, 130, 131
26:11 192

Ecclesiastes
9:5 .... 132, 134

Song of Solomon
1:4 135
1:13 135
1:17 135
2:4–6 135
3:4 135
4:1–5:1 135

Isaiah
1:2 185
2:2–5 175
3:14–15 41
6:9–10 182
7:14 176
9:1 154
11:10 175
13:22 82
14:13 114
19:3 101
26:19 161
27:1 .... 121, 122
30:27–28 70
32:7 41

32:14 98
32:14–16 154
34:1–4 159
34:11 82
34:13–14 82
34:14 82
37:16 101
37:20 101
40:3 153
42:1 154
50:6 155
51:9 121
52:7 154
53:11 155
53:12 155
56:6–7 155
60:19–20 162
61:1 154
64:1 154
66 176–77
66:18–20 175–176
66:19 176–77

Jeremiah
2:7 69
4:4 80
5:28 41
26:16–17 95
31:9 185
31:33 80
32:39 80
32:40 80

Ezekiel
1 30
1:1–4 208
4:12–13 196
11:19 80
23:45–47 95
27:12–15 139

28:13 109	**Joel**
36:26 80	2:32 76
36:27.....................................80	
37:1–10.................................. 161	**Amos**
38:2 138	2:6–7 41
38:2–3....................................138	2:10 69
38:6 138	5:12 41
38:15 138	9:11 46
39:1–2....................................138	9:11–12 44–45

Daniel

Habakkuk

4:13 .... 113, 117	3...145
4:17 .... 113, 117	3:3–4.....................................144
4:24 117	3:9–11....................................144
7–8 140	
7:9–10................................... 117	**Zechariah**
7:10 116	3:3–4.....................................195
8:13...................................... 113	5:5–8.....................................30
8:24 114	7:10 41
10 179	9:10 222
10:13 .... 179, 206	9:14.......................................145
10:21 179	12...147
11 140	12:3.......................................147
11:36–37 140	12:7–9 147
12:1 179	12:8.......................................148
12:2–3 161	12:9.......................................147
	12:9–10 148

Hosea

12:3 141	12:10 147
12:3–4 141–42	14:5.. 113

New Testament

Matthew

1:23 143	5:43–44 131
2:1–12....................................218	8:29 178–79
3:16...................................... 190	10:1–4 .... 245n2
4:1–11 ....83, 245n1	10:25..................................... 140
4:3–6................................ 178–79	12:33 78
	12:43–45.................................83

18:10 118
22:21 42
27:51–56 160
27:53 .... 243n2

Mark

1:3–4 153
1:9–11 154
1:12–13 .... 154, 245n1
1:14–15 154
1:24 158–59
2:19 136
3:13–19 .... 245n2
3:22 180
4:35–40 158
5 158–59
5:1 158
5:1–20 163
5:3–5 157
5:6–10 157
5:7 .... 158, 159
5:11–13 157–58
5:15 157
10:33–34 155
10:45 155
11:17 155
13:10 155
15:38–41 160
16 164
16:17–18 .... 163, 164, 165

Luke

6:12–15 .... 245n2
8:29 83
11:24–26 83
20:34–36 .... 244n2
23:44–49 160
24:44–47 178

John

1:1 166
1:1–3 .... 182, 186, 212
1:11 .... 244n2
1:12 206
1:14 .... 166, 167, 168, 186
1:17–18 182
1:18 .... 141, 142–43
3:29 136
4:24 144
5:4 9
8:56 186
12:8 41
12:31 .... 180, 183
12:36–37 167
14:30 .... 180, 183
16:11 .... 180, 183
17:1–26 74–75
17:6 74
17:11 75
17:11b–12a 74
17:20–21a 74
17:21 75
17:26 74
19:37 147

Acts

1:8 .... 172, 173
2 .... 42, 169–73
2:1–11 171
2:6 172
2:41 173
2:42–45 42
5 42
5:12–13 164
5:40–42 76
7:30–35 68
7:53 199
8:17–19 164
8:39–40 30

14:3 164

15 45

15:16–18 44

16:6–7 190

19:6 164

19:11 164

19:12 164

19:17 164

26:18 184

28:3–6 164

28:8 164

Romans

1:11 164

3:1–2 192

3:2 202

4 79

4:1–12 77

8:9–10 .... 245n2

8:15–23 .... 244n2

8:18–19 206

9–11 176

9:3 176

9:6–8 .... 244n2

10 76

10:9 76

10:13 76

11:7–8 182

11:25 .... 175, 176, 182

11:25–26 176

11:26 176

13:3 179

15:24 .... 174, 176

15:28 174

1 Corinthians

2:6–8 179

6:3 206

7:18 192

8:5 183

10:19–20 183

12:27–30 164–65

14:20–28 162

15:20 .... 243n2

15:20–22 162

15:23 .... 243n2

15:45–48 162

2 Corinthians

2:11 181

2:14 205

3–4 183

3:17 190

4:3–4 .... 181, 182

4:4 182

4:6 184

11:14 181

12:7 181

Galatians

2:16 77

3:7–9 .... 185, 187

3:8 186

3:9 193

3:13 93

3:19 199

3:25–29 .... 185, 187

3:26 193

3:29 193

4 198

4:1–7 198

4:3 198

4:4–6 .... 245n2

4:8–11 198

4:9 198

4:10 198

5:11–12 195

Ephesians

1:4–5 .... 244n2

1:7–9 179
1:15–23 162
1:20–21 .... 188, 226
1:21 205–6
2:1–2 183
2:8 78
2:8–9 .... 37, 77, 215
2:19–22 .... 244n2
3:3–11 179
3:10 205
4 .... 189, 203
4:8 ....188, 189
4:8–10 ....204, 205
4:8–12 225
4:9–12 189
4:11 189
5:4 196
5:8 184
5:11 184
5:22–25 136
6:11–12 226
6:12........................ 180, 184, 205

Philippians

1:19 .... 245n2
3 192
3:1–3 191
3:3 192
3:4–7.....................................196
3:8 .... 194, 195, 196
3:19..183
4:8 196

Colossians

1:11–13 .... 244n2
1:13 184
1:16 206
2.. 198
2:8 ....197, 198
2:11–12 200

2:13–15 162
2:14.......................................199
2:15.......................188, 204, 205
2:18................................. 197, 199
2:20 198
2:20–21 .... 197, 199

1 Timothy

2:5 118

2 Timothy

3:16................................207, 209

Titus

1:3–4 182

Hebrews

2:2 199
2:5–13 .... 244n2
4:16.......................................118
5:12 198

James

1:1–3.....................................215
1:17 211–12
2:6... 41
2:14–26 78
2:17..78
2:19................................214–15
2:25 96

1 Peter

1:10–11 .... 245n2
3:18–22 190
3:22 188

2 Peter

1:2–4...........................187, 244n2
1:16–21 209
2:4–5.......................... 115, 241n1

2:4–10 16
3:16 188

1 John

1:5 212
2:1 118
2:11 184
3:1 .... 244n2
3:1–3 206

Jude

5 .... 73–74, 149
6 .... 241n1
6–7 16

Revelation

2:25–27 206
2:25–28 219
2:27 219
3:21 219–20
12:1–9 221–22
12:7 222–23
12:9 115
16:14 ....147, 161
19:6–10 136
19:7 136
19:11–21 225
20:2 115
20:9 147
21–22 161
21:4 162
21:9 136
21:25 161
22:5 161
22:16 219

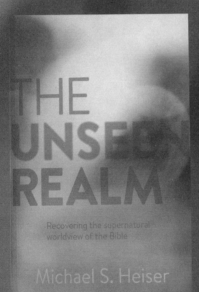